"For years I have witnessed Ron's leadersi love and wisdom. *Uniquely You* is about embracing your own journey in order to help those you serve also lead with that same love and wisdom, and to help them grow their impact and influence."

Bob Goff, author of *New York Times* bestsellers *Love Does* and *Everybody, Always*

"I've seen firsthand how Ron has lifted up an entire community of leaders in Kalamazoo, Michigan. I'm really excited that this book gives the rest of the world the opportunity to be as equipped and encouraged as I've been by his work!"

Jon Acuff, *New York Times* bestselling author of *Finish: Give Yourself the Gift of Done*

"Ron Kitchens is an extraordinary leader who inspires our dreams and shows us how to achieve them, and this book is his gift to everyone who is trying to improve themselves, their communities, and the world. *Uniquely You* is a wonderful compilation of personal stories, management advice, and leadership inspiration. Read it to discover and fulfill your true potential."

Denise Lee Yohn, brand leadership expert and bestselling author of *What Great Brands Do* and *FUSION*

"Ron Kitchens carries a joy, delight, and contagious appreciation for the world and people wherever he goes. He makes us want to be better people, live better lives, and lead with more courage. Don't miss the chance to glean from his wisdom!"

Margaret Feinberg, author of *Taste and See: An Aspiring Foodie's Search for God Among Butchers, Bakers, and Fresh Food Makers*

"Like its author, *Uniquely You* is innovative, impactful, and truly transformational. This book speaks to the power your own story has to transform your life and organization. If you miss out on this book, you do so at your own peril."

Jonathan Merritt, author of *Learning to Speak God from Scratch* and contributing writer for *The Atlantic*

"Ron Kitchens takes readers on a journey of vulnerability, honesty, and compassion. The stories he tells, which have shaped his life and his leadership, will change the lives of readers and help them discover their own unique stories that will change the trajectory of the organizations they serve."

Nancy Duarte, CEO and bestselling author

"Ron is a leader worth following. His life and leadership are packed full of wisdom, insight, know-how, and practical discernment, based on a life well-lived that includes both success and heartaches. In *Uniquely You* he openly shares many of those powerful stories, knowing they will inspire you to take your life and leadership to the next level."

Brad Lomenick, former president of Catalyst and author of *The Catalyst Leader* and *H3 Leadership*

"*Uniquely You* beautifully weaves together inspiration with practical wisdom. Ron will teach you how to lead with the freedom that only comes when you embrace your unique story. This book moved me and gave me fresh insight for my own leadership. Read this book for help to become the influential person you were created to be!"

Lucas Ramirez, author of *Designed for More* and CEO of The Gathering Place

"Learn from the master how to lead with integrity and motivate people to achieve extraordinary excellence. Ron Kitchens is a classic American rags-to-riches success story, but he doesn't stop there. He is also passionate about helping others achieve the American dream and has had a high degree of success. This book is an easy read packed with practical ideas to improve your business and your life. If you are in a position of leadership or just trolling for a business book loaded with inspirational ideas, this book is for you."

Dan Behm, former president and CEO of OST (Open Systems Technologies) and author of *Chief Culture Officer*

"However disappointing or fractured our stories may be, they have the potential to help us become the unique leaders we are meant to be in this world. In *Uniquely You* Ron shows you how to listen to your story, take stock, and move steadily into your life's calling."

Chad R. Allen, creator of Book Proposal Academy

UNIQUELY YOU

TRANSFORM YOUR
ORGANIZATION
BY BECOMING THE LEADER
ONLY YOU CAN BE

RON KITCHENS

BakerBooks
a division of Baker Publishing Group
Grand Rapids, Michigan

Published by Baker Books
a division of Baker Publishing Group
PO Box 6287, Grand Rapids, MI 49516-6287
www.bakerbooks.com

Paperback edition published 2020
ISBN 978-0-8010-9514-6

Printed in the United States of America

The Library of Congress has cataloged the original edition as follows:
Names: Kitchens, Ron, author.
Title: Uniquely you : transform your organization by becoming the leader only you can be / Ron Kitchens.
Description: Grand Rapids : Baker Books, a division of Baker Publishing Group, 2019. | Includes bibliographical references.
Identifiers: LCCN 2018053486 | ISBN 9780801093746 (cloth)
Subjects: LCSH: Leadership. | Corporate culture.
Classification: LCC HM1261 .K52 2019 | DDC 302.3/5—dc23
LC record available at https://lccn.loc.gov/2018053486

Some names and details have been changed to protect the privacy of the individuals involved.

All author proceeds from this book will be contributed to programs that embrace the belief that *the greatest force for change is a job.*

Author is represented by The Christopher Ferebee Agency, www.christopherferebee.com.

20 21 22 23 24 25 26   7 6 5 4 3 2 1

Contents

Contents

Because true belonging only happens when we present our authentic, imperfect selves to the world, our sense of belonging can never be greater than our level of self-acceptance.

Brené Brown

Author's Note

Over the past thirty-five years as a businessperson, elected official, philanthropist, economic developer, and organizational consultant, I have had the privilege of working with some of the most amazing women and men in America. This book is dedicated to them, with gratitude for the lessons they taught me. I share these lessons with you to help you lift up future leaders—especially the next generation, who I believe will be the greatest generation our planet has ever seen. Millennials, this one's for you!

You will notice that I end each chapter with sections titled "Always Forward" and "Your Unique Journey." These include questions intended to stimulate you to understand your own unique life experiences and how they can serve you, your organization, and your future on your unique journey.

Always forward,

Ron Kitchens
Lyndon Hill
Kalamazoo, Michigan
September 1, 2018

Foreword

COFFEE AND VISIONS

········· HEATHER BAKER ·········

E arly November 2006, I found myself in the job market. Or rather, life thrust me into it. Given my role as a stay-at-home mom, over the prior ten years I'd considered myself "voluntarily retired." But life's twists and turns found me about to become the divorced mother of three young children who liked to eat and to live in a warm house. It was time for my employment reentry.

Job prospects seemed dubious. I was an Ivy League graduate who had majored in history and now lived half a country away from my prior business contacts. Potential employers could easily view my decade-old experience as an organizational consultant as outdated. And workplace technology had changed a lot. On paper I appeared overqualified or underqualified, depending on who was looking.

Would anyone take a chance and hire me?

Ron Kitchens did.

His name came up during my preinterview with a Midwest staffing and recruiting firm. My interviewer informed me that Ron Kitchens at Southwest Michigan First was seeking a receptionist, and I was a potential candidate. The name didn't mean anything to me at the time, but I was told that Ron Kitchens was absolutely "awesome" and that I would love him.

Truth be told, I did not enjoy chitchatting on the phone, nor did I know how to make coffee, as I didn't drink it. Yet. But I immediately underwent a talent evaluation and discovered that my talents just might complement the Southwest Michigan First team. I met with Ron Kitchens the following week.

As I arrived at our meeting place, my nerves ascended right along with the hotel escalator. It had been fifteen years since my last job interview. Most of my conversations over the past few years had been with humans under age ten. I was led to a table where a warm and gracious gentleman stood to shake my hand. He invited me to sit. Immediately I felt at ease.

Over bacon and eggs, Ron Kitchens and I spoke at length about our past experiences, the mission of Southwest Michigan First, and what the future might hold for both of us. I explained my reservations, and he assured me that my fit with the team was most important, and that my missing skills could be taught. He liked to introduce new employees through the front desk or concierge roles. By answering the phone and greeting guests, I would learn the why, how, what, and who of the business, in preparation for other responsibilities.

Ron Kitchens quickly became Ron.

I answered my first phone call for Southwest Michigan First on January 8, 2007. The ride since then has been exciting. And unique. Ron is always leading our community and organization forward.

I'm an outsider to the Midwest and the world of economic development—both comprising the ground in which Southwest Michigan First is rooted. So I bring some objectivity in what I share. I had previously worked at for-profit companies; now I was supporting an agency with an altruistic mission. Today I am officially a raving fan.

After my first month and a half on the job, Ron approached me with an idea—the first of many—that would become his first book, *Community Capitalism: Lessons from Kalamazoo and Beyond*. It would tell the history of Southwest Michigan First and its impact on the community, the first book by a leader of an economic development organization with all profits going toward its mission: "The greatest force for change is a job." Ron had noticed that my writing was much better than my coffee, and he asked me to do research and editing for the book.

The Kalamazoo area was—in some cases, still is—the global capital of celery, paper, corsets, Upjohn Company medicines, Shakespeare rods and reels, Gibson guitars, Kellogg's Corn Flakes, Checker taxis, and Stryker knee replacements. But hard times hit in 1999. The community fell into a desperate recession even before the 2009 worldwide "Great Recession." In that last year of the twentieth century, General Motors closed its local 2.2-million-square-foot automotive stamping plant, laying off four thousand people. Six paper mills closed in the following two years, putting 1,200 more people out of work. Another seven hundred employees lost their jobs when National City merged with First of America. Perhaps most devastating was a series of mergers and acquisitions involving the Upjohn Company, Pharmacia, and Pfizer, eliminating an additional four thousand high-paying jobs.

Southwest Michigan First responded with its "community capitalism" approach, strengthening community facets of place, capital, infrastructure, talent, and education. Arriving on the scene in 2005, Ron inherited more than a few economic development projects already in the works and was tasked with:

- Filling the revamped 1.9-million-square-foot stamping plant—now known as Midlink Business Park—with manufacturing and logistics companies.
- Attracting more than fifty new and startup design, high-tech, and biopharma companies to the business campus of the Western Michigan University Business Technology and Research Park.
- Assisting over a hundred startups in a fifty-eight-thousand-square-foot life sciences incubator.

He put the Southwest Michigan First team into overdrive, attracting and retaining companies. Since then he has ensured service to more than three hundred companies and helped create thirty-eight thousand jobs. Ron found himself:

- Part of the team that crafted the Kalamazoo Promise, a revolutionary college scholarship designed by local philanthropists for public-school graduates.

12

- Senior partner of the $65 million SWMF Life Science Fund, which at the time was the largest-ever private capital fund for local economic growth, according to the *Financial Times*.
- One of twenty regional early adopters of targeted team engagement practices for strategic hiring and training.

The story spread. December 2007 found Kalamazoo, Ron, and community capitalism in the pages of *Fast Company*—the first time an economic development group appeared on the magazine's Fast 50 list. And Ron's book? Thousands of copies sold, and it became a bestseller, garnering accolades in the field of economic development and named 2008 Global Innovator by Cornet Global.

Southwest Michigan First began earning kudos for engagement practices introduced under Ron's leadership—its morning kickoff meetings, called "scrums," family-first policies, strengths-based assignments, and more—about which you'll soon read. In 2008 the *Wall Street Journal* recognized Southwest Michigan First as one of its Top Small Workplaces. In 2012 National Best and Brightest Companies to Work For picked Southwest Michigan First as its Elite Small Business, and our organization has made the list every year since. The 2016 American Business Awards rewarded Southwest Michigan First with a gold Stevie as the Non-Profit Organization of the Year. In that same year, *Outside* magazine picked the agency as one of its top three Best Places to Work. In 2017 it was certified as a Great Place to Work, and in 2018, for the seventh straight year, the organization was awarded an elite award from West Michigan's Best and Brightest Companies to Work For.

In 2009 the Southwest Michigan First board tasked Ron to come up with a plan to grow legacy leadership in the community and expand diversity of its C-level membership with respect to gender, geography, age, and industry. Ron came back with an out-of-the-box vision—a must-attend, day-long leadership conference like those offered in New York, Chicago, and Atlanta, jam-packed with top global speakers. Ron boldly challenged the team to invite bestselling authors such as Simon Sinek, Sean Achor, Nancy Duarte, Jon Acuff, and Bob Goff of *Love Does* fame. They reached out to Scott Harrison of charity: water, Lyn Heward of Cirque du Soleil, Senator Corey Booker, leadership gurus such as Patrick Lencioni and Jon Gordon, young entrepreneurs such as singer Caitlyn Crosby and Hannah Brencher, and branding expert Denise Lee Yohn. And Ron mandated that the day open to AC/DC's "Hell's Bells" blaring through the loudspeakers. "We will invite everyone we know, and thousands of people will come together to laugh, cry, sing, and be inspired," said Ron. The event was called Catalyst University.

Almost 350 people attended that first event in 2010, when Simon Sinek of *Start with Why* fame took to the stage. The next year five hundred came. By 2016 we outgrew our original venue and had to move to a hockey rink, growing to three thousand attendees in 2018. If you're interested, why don't you purchase a ticket for you and a friend to attend?

Ron introduced yet another big idea—development of a consulting unit that came to be called Consultant Connect. He was proud of the intellectual property our team had amassed on economic development, leadership development, team engagement, and organizational capacity. The time had come to share it with others. He hoped Southwest Michigan

First could become like a teaching hospital for growing the capacity of leaders like us. Initial services involved custom events around the United States to connect economic developers with site consultants, then grew to accommodate programs built around the expertise of our team of consultants. In 2011 Consultant Connect serviced almost twenty external clients, and today more than three hundred groups engage annually at tailored events around the country.

As time moved forward, community stories, Southwest Michigan First strategies, and Ron continued to find themselves featured extensively in national and international media outlets, including the *Wall Street Journal*, *Fast Company*, CBS, NBC, Fox, *USA Today*, *Forbes*, *Fortune*, the *Economist*, and National Public Radio. But as the global economy changed, news outlets downsized, merged, or closed their doors. So instead of waiting for others to tell the region's news, Ron wondered, why not draw again upon the skills of the team—this time in writing, in coordination with other news sources—and do the unthinkable: start a business magazine? Yes, at a time when many print periodicals were failing, he bucked the trend and started the bimonthly, high-gloss, locally focused *269 Magazine*. More than sixty advertisers showed up, as well as news stories—Ron loves a good story!—featuring 420 companies and 247 leaders in over 140,000 copies. Readers can sense his oversight as publisher on every page.

We see much to celebrate in Southwest Michigan. In 2017 and 2018 alone, plans for $1.35 billion of investment have been announced in Kalamazoo and the greater Southwest Michigan region. Chief among them are expansions at Pfizer and Stryker, bolstered by Southwest Michigan First's economic development services. Pfizer will be constructing a $465 million, state-of-the-art medications facility—one of the most technologically advanced operations of its kind in the world. Stryker is investing $110 million in its Portage facility, which will lead to the creation of 260 high-paying jobs by 2025. These follow a recent multimillion-dollar expansion of Newell Brands at its design and testing facility in Kalamazoo, after its 2013 attraction announcement to the area's design-centric workforce. These are just three of over twenty current or recent major projects in the community that have kept the jobless rate below 4.5 percent and at times as low as 3 percent—well below the region's historical average—over the past two years.

Along with state and local government investment, over the years Ron and Southwest Michigan First have brought together dedicated corporate, community, and civic partners again and again to encourage successful outcomes. The Southwest Michigan First board has grown to a dynamic and nimble sixty-some members—men and women who lead Fortune 500 and other great companies with roots in Southwest Michigan. For its expansion, Pfizer was the first to take advantage of the Good Jobs for Michigan program, signed into law by Governor Rick Snyder and championed by Southwest Michigan First. The attraction of Newell Brands to Southwest Michigan precipitated the creation of the Richmond Institute of Product Design and Innovation at Western Michigan University to further address corporate demand for product design and engineering skills. The organization saw opportunity for greater community alignment as it passed ownership of its life science incubator to the Western Michigan University Homer Stryker M.D.

School of Medicine. Respected partnerships and outcomes like these led the governor to appoint Ron as trustee of the Kalamazoo-based research university.

Things like these do not happen by accident when Ron Kitchens is around. They are unprecedented achievements brought to fruition through calculated strategy and focused efforts.

Ron and I have become great coworkers, partners, catapulters, cheerleaders, and friends since that fateful day in 2006. I thank him most for helping me find my own unique self. I believe by this book's end you will too.

And in case you're wondering, I can make a good cup of coffee now. Keurig makes it easy.

0

Changed for Good

LIVING YOUR TRUTH

> Incredible change happens in your life when you decide to take control of what you do have power over instead of craving control over what you don't.
>
> Steve Maraboli

The first forty years of my life I spent terrified that people would discover the truth about me. That I was a phony, a fraud, not the person they assumed me to be. This fear both drove me to succeed and left me paralyzed. What if people found out that all they knew of my life was a highlight reel? I had never shared the truth with anyone—not my closest friends, not even my wife.

But all of that changed one brisk autumn evening in 2003 at Manhattan's Gershwin Theatre. I had heard that *Wicked* was one of the best shows on Broadway. I had never gone to a Broadway show before, but I had some time to kill, so why not? For those unfamiliar, the musical is the origin story of the witches of Oz, long before Dorothy would arrive in her tornado-borne house. One of the characters, Elphaba, has green skin. The audience knows that she is destined to become the Wicked Witch of the West, but she starts out a good witch. As the first act unfolds, she begins to grow angry that she has to put on a front to appear normal and earn the affection of her peers.

The dam holding back Elphaba's emotions breaks in the first act's final song, "Defying Gravity," in which she sings about limits others place on her because of their perceptions of her. She finishes by stating that their approval comes at too high a cost.

Intermission began, the song's words still echoing throughout the theatre. I sat with tears streaming down my cheeks, crying over a song about a green witch. I'm not talking about national-anthem crying or I-can't-believe-I-am-a-father crying. This was deep, guttural, ugly crying. The only other time I ever cried tears like that was upon the death of my grandfather.

This was a story I had never heard before. Yet I had known it my whole life.

I was Elphaba. Green and different. I was unlike my peers, but I knew that somewhere others must have a similar history.

My story began when two teenagers ran away to Mexico to get married because they were far too young to do so in California. My mother was not even old enough to drive when I was born. She was so scared that she lied about her age on my birth certificate for fear that the hospital would call Child

Protective Services or, worse yet, her father. I wish that were the worst of it. The plot grows darker with the intrusion of learning disabilities, abuse, family mental illness, poverty, and, in the end, my crippling fear of being discovered as a fraud.

When I had walked into the Gershwin Theatre that night, all of these unsightly details had been safely tucked away for decades, painted over with a veneer of marketplace success and respectability. I had been traveling the country speaking at sold-out conferences and leading a multimillion-dollar organization. I lived in a luxurious house on a golf course with my all-American family.

But I was a walking paradox. I was surrounded by Ivy League graduates; it had taken me eight years to graduate from state college. My friends were from families of influence and education; I was the dyslexic son of a dyslexic father who never learned to read. As an adult I had achieved financial wealth. But as a child I had climbed inside a Goodwill donation box to steal school clothes.

During intermission at the Gershwin I struggled to regain my composure. Throughout the second act my mind spun. Sitting there, I realized that life—with its journeys, struggles, and main characters—is always speaking to us. It is telling us who we are, who we are not, and who we are meant to be. Our stories shape who we are. We cannot escape them; we can only embrace them.

I walked out of the theatre a new man that night. No longer would I carry a suitcase of shame about the story that formed me. No longer would I live in fear that people would discover my past. No longer would I harbor anger at those who hurt me. It was time to stop running from my story and start listening to my life.

But living that commitment—a transparent life, setting aside old fears—proved to be an even more difficult journey. Living fearlessly is a muscle that has to be developed daily.

As I have looked back on my past and present, I have realized that they are inextricably linked. Each of us has lessons that life is trying to teach us. But we must listen without judgment and self-loathing. We must embrace our unique stories and let them shape us as fathers and mothers, husbands and wives, entrepreneurs and business leaders. In fact, these last two roles are the reason this book exists—to show how my past life experiences have revolutionized my leadership, often without me even realizing it. I want to teach you also how your story can transform you into what only you can be, the unique leader your organization needs.

1

Mandarin Oranges

A SMALL GIFT CAN CHANGE A LIFE

From now on, any definition of a successful life
must include serving others.

George H. W. Bush

I was born with a black eye and a hole in my neck, leaving
scars both visible and invisible that I still carry today.

At ages fourteen and fifteen, respectively, my parents went
to Mexico to marry. Neither had attended high school, and
they had little or no family support. My mother, Judy, was
fifteen when I was born. She and my sixteen-year-old father,
Ron, were beginning their family that February day—two
kids about to have a kid.

My mom and I nearly died at my birth. Forceps were used,
damaging my neck, face, and sinuses. But the forceps ultimately saved both our lives.

In all of this my mom wasn't just running away; she was
deciding to start her own life. To this day she's one of the

23

bravest people I know. She has always encouraged my brother, John, and me to succeed, even when she could not define success or describe what it could look like.

My father quit school at twelve to work and support his mother and sister after his father unexpectedly died. Then my father died at twenty, when I was only four. One of my few memories of him is him coming home, covered in soot and grease, from his job at a foundry, where he was killed. I also remember one time waiting in terror in my room for his arrival after I threw a rock at the neighbor kid and caused him to need stitches. My father didn't punish me but told me we didn't have money for the child's medical bills, and for that I should be ashamed. I will never forget feeling ashamed because we were poor and because I was responsible for the physical and financial pain of others.

I also remember the day my father died. One of his friends came to my grandfather's house sobbing inconsolably, saying my dad was the kindest man he'd ever known.

My father died because he was illiterate; he never received the education to overcome the dyslexia we share. Because of his lack of education and his commitment to his young family, he had to take a dangerous job, where he made a mistake that cost him his life. I'm sure there was a warning sign somewhere, but signs matter little if you can't read. At nineteen my mother found herself a widow with two children, little family support, and a bleak future.

● ● ●

Crack, crack, crack, came the knock on the door. No one would have guessed its impact and the exceptional life that would start that Christmas Day.

As usual, we didn't answer the door. Unexpected knocks never meant anything good in our house. Usually it indicated bill collectors or those like the man who repossessed an accordion my mom had bought for my brother and me. This day, however, I snuck to the window and watched as three strange men left a banana box on our porch. I can still remember, with a clarity that has not diminished with time, looking at each item as we unpacked the box with a sense of awe and wonder. But one item captured my attention and held it: a can of mandarin oranges. It probably cost less than a quarter at that time, but in the Missouri Ozarks in the 1970s tropical fruit (canned or not) was rare and special, to be saved for an occasion equally as special.

Because of how special that can of oranges was, it was placed in the kitchen cabinet to be saved for a special occasion. For months, it sat there just staring at me. When I would retrieve cereal, that can would catch my eye. When I would reach for a can of soup, I would see those oranges. Whenever the cabinet opened, I saw that can and remembered that someone cared for me. The men who dropped off that box did not know us. They came from a church we did not attend. But that can of mandarin oranges became an emblem of others' concern for me. On the nights I felt scared or lonely, that can gave me peace, hope, and the determination to find a better life. It reminded me that I was not alone and never forgotten, that for some reason someone out there loved me.

We did not stay in that house for long. In fact, we did not stay in any house for very long. Our family was stuck in a cycle. We moved into a home until the bills stacked up too high to ignore. In a rush, we then gathered our belongings

25

and fled. Anyone who grew up poor can attest to this process. Whenever you're moving to a new place, there is an unspoken hierarchy that is attached to your things. Toys are at the bottom, and they are always left behind. Food is always at the top of the chain, and it is packed first. For many years, that can of oranges followed us from pantry to pantry, house to house. We were saving it for an occasion that was special enough to justify its consumption, but that day never came. Instead, those oranges became a symbol of the Christmas when food had miraculously appeared. The can bloated over time, and my mother finally threw it away, which left an empty space on the shelf and a gap in my sense of security.

After what I am sure was an overabundance of whining, my mom returned from the grocery store one day with a new can of mandarin oranges. This time, however, the oranges did not go into the kitchen cabinet. Instead, my mom told me to put the can on my "desk"—a rusted, formerly orange TV tray—as a reminder of the cost of a lack of education and that there were good people in the world who cared about more than just themselves.

Every desk I have called my own from that day forward has had a can of mandarin oranges placed inside it. It was there when I graduated from high school, there throughout my college years. Today, there is a can in all three of the desks in the three offices I call my own.

I have founded multiple companies, served hundreds of communities, been elected to office, and sat on the corporate boards of more than twenty organizations. Throughout those years that can of oranges has been with me as an emblem of my responsibility to grow new leaders and has catapulted me to new heights. When I grow discouraged and am tempted to give up, that can calls to me from inside my desk drawer, *Never quit, Ron. You are not alone, you were never forgotten. You are loved, you are worthy.* I have achieved more than I ever believed possible, and that can of oranges has become more than a symbol of education and escaping poverty. It is my daily reminder of the responsibility I have to serve others. To pay forward the gift I received as a child. If I could commit to a tattoo, it would be of a can of mandarin oranges.

Whenever I hire a new employee, I sneak into their office and place a can of mandarin oranges on their desk. The primary color of our leadership division, which teaches and grows more than three thousand leaders annually, is orange. In 2017 we had a limited edition beer brewed that was called Catalyst Mandarin Orange.

The story of that can of oranges is not just sentimental; it is the foundation of my leadership journey.

Since I launched my first company thirty-six years ago at age nineteen, I have had the privilege to consult and coach thousands of leaders—from small businesses to Fortune 500 CEOs, US Senators to faith leaders. The men and women with whom I have the pleasure to work believe that they are created to achieve greatness, but they are often exhausted, disenchanted, and overwhelmed. One reason for this stems from our quick-fix culture. It seems that every book, podcast, and TED video promises a magic bullet, a get-rich-quick scheme, or the recipe for secret sauce. And around every corner stands a fire-walking guru who promises to show you the shortcut to success—for a price. Leaders buy into these lies only to realize later that the promises were empty and the predictions didn't pan out.

Here's the good news: you already have what you need to succeed. But you must muster the courage to excavate it, embrace it, and share it. Every person I have ever worked with has been given a set of stories, life experiences, and relationships, regardless of their age, gender, culture, or religion. Each of these experiences, good and bad, is a gift from which the leader can learn. Our stories possess the power to grow us into better leaders than we might otherwise become. Those who embrace their unique stories have unique success.

ALWAYS FORWARD

- Who can you serve today to change their life—or simply show love and compassion—with something as basic as a box of food or a can of oranges?

YOUR UNIQUE JOURNEY

You are welcome to apply my mandarin orange lesson in your life, or maybe your life story wants to teach you something more important for this moment. On pages 201–8 I've provided a brainstorming tool titled "Mining Lessons from Your Unique Life Story," a list of categories and prompts to help you remember instructive stories and experiences from your past. What is your life trying to teach you?

2

"You Can't Read"

BOOKS, GROWTH, AND SUCCESS

Little children, let us not love with word or with
tongue, but in deed and truth.

1 John 3:18

You cannot read," said Mrs. Names, "and you do not
know your alphabet." Even as a second grader, I knew
this was a problem.

Mrs. Names had asked me to stay in at recess to talk. The
truth is, it wasn't unusual for me to be asked to stay after
class, but this time was different. After the room cleared out
and the noise of my excited classmates retreated down the
hall, I remained at my desk as Mrs. Names took up a chair
next to me. She looked at me seriously for a moment, then
told me bluntly that I was falling far behind. She told me that,
since I didn't know the alphabet, I had little hope of reading

alongside my classmates. But Mrs. Names also told me that, if I were willing to stay in for recess each day to practice with her, I could catch up with the class. I remember initially being embarrassed but also happy that an adult wanted to spend time with me. Looking back, I see she was making a bigger sacrifice than I realized—she was giving up some of her rare free time to make a difference for one child. I have never been a second-grade teacher, but I am fairly sure that recess was invented by one of them to escape second-grade boys.

For months Mrs. Names taught me, and I improved gradually. Eventually we were able to read whole books together during recess. This continued until one day my mom showed up in my classroom and told me to gather my belongings—we had to move again. This would be school number seven for me.

I was devastated, but before I left the room, Mrs. Names squatted down, looked me in the eye, and whispered, "You are a reader. Read everything you can, as much as you can, and one day you *will* go to college." What an amazing vision for a child's life.

My family moved a lot; I attended thirteen schools before the sixth grade. Thankfully, we bounced between only California and Missouri. I say thankfully because Ozark, Missouri, was my grandfather's hometown, and it boasted an exceptional library—the Christian County Library—and a librarian I knew well, Frieda Sweet.

Frieda had gone to school with my grandfather, and they were good friends. Mrs. Names may have taught me to read, but Frieda taught me to love books. She showed me how to be inquisitive with books, to be a collector of the stories they told.

I would regularly visit the library and wander around; it was my favorite place to go for quiet and air-conditioning. We never had air-conditioning at home, so the library was especially attractive in summer. I usually had it to myself. And when I would return books, Frieda would respond, "Oh, I was just thinking of you." And she would reach for a small stack of books she'd set aside for me to read next. I vividly remember Frieda often asking what I thought was important in the stories. She did much more than check books in and out; Frieda loved the stories, and she taught me to discover their magic for myself.

I remember returning *The Adventures of Huckleberry Finn* when Frieda said, "You know our river, the Finley River, goes all the way to the Mississippi, right?"

I rebutted, "No, it doesn't!"

But she said, "No, look!" and pulled out maps to show me how the Finley flowed into the James River, which spilled into the White River, which in turn wound its way through the countryside to join the Mississippi, which we then followed all the way to New Orleans. The idea that I had a real-life connection to those stories brought them to life for me in a way that I still embrace today.

These two strong women created in me a passion for reading, and I have made it a life priority ever since. I have also incorporated reading into my team's strategy for success at Southwest Michigan First, based on our belief that high-performance teams are well read. Reading the same books as a team helps build a common strategy and a common vocabulary, it closes the knowledge gap between team members of different ages and backgrounds, and it challenges our processes and provokes thoughtful questions.

● ● ●

According to the Pew Research Center, the average person reads four books per year. But highly successful people, such as CEOs, read twenty-five to fifty books per year.[1] Why do these ultra-busy men and women read so voraciously, as though their careers depend on it? Because they do. Organizations are either going to improve or decline, but nothing ever stays the same. Pouring knowledge into your people by reading together is a critical strategy to ensure that your organization is continuously improving.

An old adage says, "The man who does not read good books has no advantage over the man who cannot read them."[2] I couldn't agree more. In a country where more than 24 percent of American adults do not read a single book over the course of a year, it should be easy to stay ahead of the curve.[3] If your team is to thrive, its members must continue their education through active, lifelong learning. It's not an exaggeration to say that Mrs. Names's coaching went a long way toward making me a leader.

At Southwest Michigan First we agree that each of us is responsible for our individual education and development, and we've established numerous ways to help team members learn and grow. A leader can sit on a bulldozer all day, but unless you add fuel to the tank, it isn't going to go anywhere. It's up to each of us to fuel our leadership tanks with knowledge.

Charlie Munger, vice chairman of Berkshire Hathaway, is clear about his belief in reading: "In my whole life, I have known no wise people who didn't read all the time—none, zero." He goes on to say that the single biggest failing of CEOs is that "they do not read enough."[4] Keep in mind that Charlie Munger is interacting with the best CEOs in the world, the ones who are already reading more than fifty books per year.

At least six times each year our entire team participates in a book club—a critical part of the culture at Southwest Michigan First. To make sure our book club is engaging for all team members, we meet for breakfast to dive into deep discussion about each book. Each meeting is led by a different team member, who creates discussion questions or highlights key takeaways.

Reading and sharing together brings new team members up to speed with the basic knowledge the team shares. Along with our latest book club selections, each new member is provided copies of all books on our booklist (below), and they are expected to read the complete list during their first year at Southwest Michigan First.

Southwest Michigan First's Catalyst Reading List

- *Good to Great: Why Some Companies Make the Leap and Others Don't* by Jim Collins
- *StrengthsFinder 2.0* by Tom Rath
- *The Ideal Team Player: How to Recognize and Cultivate the Three Essential Virtues* by Patrick Lencioni
- *The Four Obsessions of an Extraordinary Executive: A Leadership Fable* by Patrick Lencioni
- *Start with Why: How Great Leaders Inspire Everyone to Take Action* by Simon Sinek
- *The 7 Habits of Highly Effective People: Powerful Lessons in Personal Change* by Stephen R. Covey

- *Community Capitalism: Lessons from Kalamazoo and Beyond* by Ron Kitchens
- *Blue Ocean Strategy: How to Create Uncontested Market Space and Make the Competition Irrelevant* by W. Chan Kim and Renée Mauborgne
- *If You Give a Mouse a Cookie* by Laura Joffe Numeroff and Felicia Bond

Now, I've been using the word *read*, but we are impartial about the method by which someone consumes the content. We give our team access to print, digital, or audio book versions. Audio in particular is a great way to consume books; my daily twenty-five-minute commute to work allows me to "read" an additional two books per month.

You can see my list of what I believe are the hundred or so most important books for leaders at www.ronkitchens .com.

ALWAYS FORWARD

- When did someone cast a vision for your life? How did that impact your future?
- Reflect on a teacher, coach, or other influential adult who impacted your life, and send her or him a thank-you. If you don't know where to send it, post it on Facebook; chances are good you'll connect. How can you pay forward that person's kindness?

- The most common excuse for not reading is lack of time. What can you eliminate or reduce in your schedule to give yourself five hours a month to read?
- Leaders of some of America's greatest organizations read a book per week. What is your plan to grow by reading? What books will you read in the next ninety days?

YOUR UNIQUE JOURNEY

My lesson about reading might be just what you need right now. Or maybe your story is trying to teach you something more pertinent in this moment. You can use the instrument provided on pages 201–8 to remind you of instructive stories and experiences from your past.

3

Lunch Shaming

CHOOSE SOLUTIONS THAT LIFT UP

No man can cause more grief than that one cling-
ing blindly to the vices of his ancestors.

William Faulkner

Like a lot of kids who grew up in poverty, I received free lunches from my school cafeteria. This happened in school after school as my family kept moving around. Whenever I changed schools, I had to adapt quickly because each had different procedures to follow. In fourth grade I started midyear at a new elementary school in California's Sierra Nevada. Each day students were given a meal ticket for that day's lunch, which they then traded for their meal. Everyone received a white ticket except the kids who got free lunch; our tickets were yellow.

A wave of embarrassment washed over me as I received my ticket and slowly realized that my classmates were whispering about that new kid and how he got free lunch. By this time I knew that on my first day my classmates were going to judge the new kid; they would try to figure me out. And my fourth-grade mind already knew what conclusion they would draw. I was all too aware that any new student had a steep hill to climb before reaching acceptance. And mine would now be steeper.

Coming from a different region and climate, my clothes were obviously not right. And since I was starting midway through the year, I already stuck out. But now my yellow lunch ticket gave my peers another reason to see I was different. I wasn't just the new kid—I was the poor new kid.

After that first day I pretended to be sick when lunchtime came around. I soon made this part of my daily routine—every day I would feign illness, forcing my teacher to send me to the nurse's office. The nurse never found anything wrong, but I made sure to sit there just long enough to avoid the lunch line. I would rather go hungry than be humiliated.

One day the principal made a surprise visit to the nurse's office to find out what was really going on. I remember breaking down in tears, confessing that my only ailment was hunger. In fact, at that point in my life I was probably also missing breakfast some days. My mother did not get up when my brother and I did, so we ate whatever we could grab as we rushed out the door. Sometimes this meant grabbing a piece of bread. Maybe there was cereal, and maybe there was nothing. I was used to being resourceful, but I could not bear the shame of the lunch line no matter how hungry I was.

Hearing my predicament, the principal, instead of doing the smart thing—the adult thing, changing the color of the school's lunch tickets—suggested that I volunteer in the kitchen serving lunch to earn my meal. I hadn't expected to be accommodated, so I took him up on his offer. Rather than receive free lunch and eat with the rest of the fourth graders, I would leave class early, put on my hairnet and apron, and serve food to my classmates. I ate my lunch after all the other students had been served, and I ate in the kitchen by myself.

This was, at the time, a point of pride for me. I would think, *I never took their charity. I worked for my meals.* Later the memory of my fourth-grade job forged a commitment in my life that I was never going to put other people in a situation where they had to be embarrassed for receiving a hand up, as I had been. We leaders must create systems that serve people without inadvertently stigmatizing them.

Frankly, I'm not sure whether the principal cared whether I ate lunch or not. I suspect he just didn't want me hanging out at the nurse's office every day and came up with a quick solution to get rid of me. He couldn't know this incident would become formative in my life. It taught me to remember that, while not everyone starts in the same place, we leaders are responsible to give everyone equal opportunities to thrive. The principal's solution did not achieve this. If I was serving lunch to my classmates, I obviously did not have the same opportunities they had.

I wish my story was unique, but the problem of lunchroom shaming continues to be an issue in America. It is so prevalent that New Mexico banned the practice, and I recently read about a school in Alabama that sent children home with an ink stamp on their arms that said, "I Need Lunch Money."[1]

• • •

To become a smarter leader I must be able to find solutions that aren't just expedient but that solve all relevant problems, including that of protecting human dignity. I'm sure other kids at my school were also humiliated by the yellow free lunch tickets. The colored tickets were a system created by indifferent adults. The color-coding may have expedited the school's accounting, but it did not serve to lift people up. Leaders in today's world need to think through the systems they establish, creating them with the intention of serving people, not processes.

It's not just bureaucracies that make bad decisions, preferring processes over people. When I was a kid, the circus came to my hometown. In retrospect I know it was a shabby show with one tent, but on that day, it was the greatest circus in the world and, as far as I can tell, the first and last one that came to town in my lifetime. The downside was that I had no way to buy myself a seat, let alone one for my brother. So I marched myself down to the city park and asked the man in charge for a job for the day, with two tickets as payment. He gave me two duties: wipe down all the folding bleachers and wash the elephant. The bleachers were easy. The elephant? Not a normal chore for a rural Missouri kid.

As I was introduced to the elephant, two things struck me—how big she was and that the only thing preventing her mad dash around the city square was a tiny rope attached to her ankle. When I questioned my qualifications and the safety of washing such a magnificent animal, I was told, "Don't worry. It's just like washing a car. And she will not break the rope. She could, but she won't. She couldn't break it as a baby, and she's given up trying."

I washed her with a sense of sadness that anything so regal could be held back by beliefs imposed on her by adults who did not have her best interests in mind.

How do we know what those ropes are in our lives? I surveyed my teammates and a few trusted leaders for answers to this question, and the consensus was that we can't answer it by ourselves. We need the insight of others to see what we can't. So ask the people who know you—your trusted advisors, your family, the people you work with.

Never be held back by the dictates of others; break the rope. And never impose such dictates on others.

ALWAYS FORWARD

- We all have ropes that bind us to old beliefs and self-limiting behavior. What ropes can you cut to gain the freedom to live your unique journey?
- Where in your organization or community are people being held back by rules that perhaps once served a need but now do more harm than good? How can you work to realign these rules?

YOUR UNIQUE JOURNEY

You are welcome to apply my lunch shaming lesson in your life, or maybe your story wants to teach you something more important for this moment. On pages 201–8 I've provided a list of categories and prompts that might help you brainstorm and remember instructive stories and experiences.

4

Pork Chops

GROWING BY OBSERVING

Education is a progressive discovery of our own ignorance.

Will Durant

I did not have many role models who could steer me in the right direction. I was in the dark about almost everything, including educational decisions, career opportunities, and even common manners. One story that sticks out to me took place in high school, when my then-girlfriend invited me to her house for dinner.

Her mom had prepared pork chops. While the rest of the table placed their napkins on their laps and reached for their utensils, I picked the meat up with my hands and started eating it straight off the bone. I had no idea this was inappropriate—this was how I had always eaten pork chops

41

in my home. The rule was, if it had a bone, use your hands. After dinner her father, a successful businessperson, kindly pulled me aside to tell me that eating with one's hands was not appropriate behavior at his table. I was mortified. Even now the memory of that moment makes my stomach turn.

I have been blessed with people who've appeared unexpectedly in my life to serve as guides and mentors. Some have traveled with me for a season; others have been constants through my life. One of those constants has been Carole Collins, the mother of my boyhood best friend, Cameron. A few days after the pork chop incident I explained my embarrassment to Carole, and she counseled me to always be an observer. She told me whenever I found myself in a new situation to first observe what others around me were doing— especially successful people—and learn from them. That guidance helped me become a lifelong learner, soaking up knowledge and experiences throughout my life and waiting just a beat or two in new situations to understand the rules.

Since then several of my most trusted mentors have given me essentially the same advice: watch what successful people do and use that to inform your decisions. Watch where they send their children to school, where they invest their money, the charities they support, and how they relax. When you grow up in a world of ignorance—and I do not mean that pejoratively—you understand that ignorance is an enemy. Ignorant people are almost never successful, impactful, or blessed.

The shocking thing about ignorance is that, even in a world where practically all knowledge is available through a smartphone, it is still incredibly difficult to recognize what we don't know. We're all guilty of being unaware of our own areas of ignorance. Leaders are rarely afraid to ask questions but often don't know the right questions to ask.

The best way to learn and improve is to put yourself in new, unfamiliar situations and to always pay attention through all your senses. Be willing to learn from anyone and any opportunity and always assume you don't already have all the answers. There's always more to know, and it's up to you to learn.

That's why the simple act of observation has served me time and again. Vigilance can spare you embarrassment, and it helps you set goals by watching for guideposts that lead toward success.

Soon after receiving Carole's advice to become an observer, I decided to combat my ignorance any way I could. Being from a small town in the Ozarks, it was easy for me to feel cut off from the rest of the world—a world that seemed to move on without me. I remember taking a school trip to what was then Southwest Missouri State University and picking up a Sunday copy of the *New York Times* in the library. I sat down in the aisle and examined this newspaper that I had never seen before. While my classmates hung out in the student union, I discovered a publication that would change my life.

More specifically, I discovered the wedding announcement section and became fascinated by the stories of the couples. I was riveted by the ways they met, the colleges they attended, their majors, and their subsequent careers. What captivated me most was that this, the nation's most prominent newspaper, had considered these people special enough to select and feature them. What made their stories unique? What could I learn from their stories to change my life?

Nearly every Sunday I still read the *New York Times.* I often disagree with the opinions in its editorial section, but that's not why I read it. Since ignorance is my enemy, I want to hear all sides of an issue. And to this day, nearly forty years later, I never skip the wedding announcements. This exercise has become a weekly moment of mentoring for life, and the newspaper serves as another of my leadership coaches. Simply by being open to learning from the lives of significant people, I can use that knowledge to improve my life and the lives of those around me. As my wife and I helped our daughter, Kelsey, choose her college, we returned to this section to track people with careers Kelsey thought were interesting. We examined how they got their starts, the companies they worked for, and the schools they'd attended.

● ● ●

My family loves the beach, but no matter how articulate I am, I can never truly describe it. You have to experience it in person. If your own eyes have never seen waves pound the beach, if you've never tasted their salty spray, if you've never felt your feet move as a wave retreats and the sand settles, it's hard for me to describe that to you. You can see it in videos or read about it, but that can't come close to the complete experience of being there. I believe in being an observer, but I've also discovered that just observing is not enough. You must also be an explorer. You must put yourself in positions to observe new ideas, customs, people, food . . . the list is endless. As Mark Twain said, "Travel is fatal to prejudice, bigotry, and narrow-mindedness, and many of our people need it sorely on these accounts. Broad, wholesome, charitable views of men and things cannot be acquired by vegetating in one little corner of the earth all one's lifetime."[1] I have studied what he meant, and it's clear he was talking about bias—specifically the biases that hold us back, that allow us to believe everyone eats pork chops with their hands.

I have to admit I'm a sucker for buddy movies. One of my favorites is *The Bucket List*, the title phrase referring to a list of things the main characters want to do before they die or "kick the bucket." While I love the movie, focusing on dying has never appealed to me. I prefer to be intentional about choosing and writing down my life goals and then purposefully achieving them. My list, which I call "A Curated Life," is informed by the choices and experiences of people I observe whom I believe to be well rounded and successful. Today my list contains more than a hundred items, each a planned experience intended to lift the fog of ignorance and make me a better person, leader, or family member.

Here's a sampling from A Curated Life:

- Talk with Academy Award–winning writer Aaron Sorkin about his creative process.
- Have dinner with Oprah Winfrey to talk about how she achieves so much in one day.
- Give a college commencement speech.
- Tour the Mississippi Blues Trail, where so much of America's music and food culture started.
- Feed ten thousand people a holiday meal over my lifetime (I'm well on my way).
- Assist sixty men and women to become leaders of their own organizations.

45

When you start your leadership journey, you will inevitably encounter your own plate of pork chops. And, as was true for me, chances are you will have no idea you just made a shocking faux pas. (That's French for "What were you thinking?") At Southwest Michigan First we refer to these teachable moments as "Lessons from behind the Boardroom Door"—lessons you can only learn if you're in the room or if someone intentionally teaches you.

It may seem a contradiction that a book about being unique would focus on observing what others do and imitating them. But just as a map helps plot your route, looking to others can help you get started in a general direction. Then, once on your way, you can make strategic adaptations, take detours, and make discoveries that allow you to map your unique journey.

Leadership is rarely linear, and it often leads into uncharted territory. As we grow, we don't always know which steps will reach our goal. Once you begin a commitment of conscious exploring, it's important not to be satisfied by your first few discoveries. New Zealand was first mapped by Dutch explorer Abel Tasman, who went on to find Tasmania and Mauritius, a speck of land in the Indian Ocean. But he completely missed Australia, the largest island in the world. If Tasman had quit after those early discoveries, he would likely be a footnote in history. But he didn't quit, and a few years later he landed on Australia's northwest coast.

ALWAYS FORWARD

- What is your pork chop story? How do its lessons inform your life? What assumptions, born of ignorance, are holding you back?
- Who are three people you can ask for honest feedback about ways lack of knowledge is limiting your success? (Who can you help in this way?)
- Which experiences can you curate for your life in order to evaporate ignorance and biases?
- How are you putting yourself into situations of discovery?

YOUR UNIQUE JOURNEY

You are welcome to apply my pork chop lesson in your life. But take a moment to listen to your life. Pages 201–8 might help you see and hear an even more important lesson on your unique journey.

5

Legacy

IMPACTING PEOPLE'S LIVES

As leaders, we are never responsible to fill anyone else's cup. Our responsibility is to empty ours.

Andy Stanley

We heard a knock on our farmhouse door. I say "our," but it really belonged to the man who was knocking, our landlord, Mr. Countryman. From the window I could see him standing on our step with the usual rectangular carpenter's pencil stuck in the pocket of his pin-striped overalls. Mr. Countryman was a cattleman and carpenter. This old farmhouse was tucked in a far corner of his property.

When my mother answered the door, Mr. Countryman came right out with it: "I notice you all do not go to church, and I would love to invite you to attend mine."

We were not church attenders. Prayer was something you did at halftime of football games if your team was down, Easter was all about colored eggs and chocolate bunnies, and Santa Claus was the reason to celebrate Christmas. I was nine then, and I don't believe I'd ever been in a church. The first Bible I owned had been given to me a year before, when I was in the third grade, not by a family member or friend but by Gideons International outside my school's entrance. I still have it today—a little green-covered New Testament.

My mother patiently allowed Mr. Countryman to finish, but church and God were simply not part of her plan for our family. My mother responded as I'd expected: "No, I really do not think I can get up and do that every week."

Our landlord's next words changed my life forever. "Well, I can understand that. But how about your sons coming?"

From that point forward, Mr. Countryman showed up at our door every Sunday morning to pick up John and me and take us to Mount Zion Southern Baptist Church. It was Mr. Countryman who bought the little white shirt I wore as I walked into the Finley River to be baptized. And it was Mr. Countryman who ensured my brother and I went to church summer camp. He made sure we not only attended church but were also there for Sunday school and understood the lessons and how they applied to our lives.

That day he showed up at our door was not National Adopt-an-Urchin Day. Mr. Countryman was simply living out a personal commitment to his faith. No matter where we moved—we changed houses about every six months—he or another member of the congregation made sure my brother and I were in Mount Zion's pews.

I think this exemplifies our obligation as leaders to lead and serve even when it isn't glamorous. There was nothing exciting about dragging two poor kids to church every Sunday. There was no banquet held in Mr. Countryman's honor. He received no trophy. In fact, it cost him valuable resources—both time and money—but he believed that living out his purpose was the most important thing he could do.

Do we leaders serve this way? Are we willing to lay down our selfish ambitions occasionally to help people when there is no return on our investment? Though Mr. Countryman did not live to see it, I've grown to be a better man because of his selfless service. In the same way, we leaders owe the same to our people, even if we don't always get to witness the fruit of our efforts. Our job is to buoy their development with helium, to pour in high expectations, to supply opportunities and tools, and to watch our teams soar. We each need to give direction to those around us, to create a little wind to help them forward. The cost to us is minimal, but the reward for the receiver is immeasurable.

● ● ●

If I asked people to name a Legacy Leader—a person who has significantly changed other people's lives—most would give names of famous or wealthy people. No one would mention Maggie Terry.

Full disclosure: Maggie was my mother-in-law. She was in my life for nearly twenty-five years, and while I always appreciated her love of family—especially her grandchildren—I never knew the impact she had on lives outside the family.

After she passed away, when her friends and family had gathered to place her remains next to her beloved husband's, we were overwhelmed by the outpouring of love and support. I was particularly surprised by two stories that none of her children had known—stories that confirmed that Maggie was indeed a Legacy Leader of the rarest kind.

As we stood in the St. Louis sunshine, a distinguished-looking woman—whom we'd never met nor heard of—approached to share her Maggie story. She explained in great detail how she'd traveled across the nation to say goodbye to Maggie. She wept as she told us that Maggie had mentored her for a decade, culminating when the woman became provost at a major university. "She set higher goals for me than I set for myself," she said between tears.

The second story belonged to a man who was once a ninth-grade history teacher. By his own admission he'd been so unhappy with his life and career choice that he'd intended to quit teaching entirely. But after a kind word from Maggie and her insistence that he apply to graduate school at Harvard, of all places, he went on to become a dean at an Ivy League university. "She believed in me when I did not believe in myself," he said.

It's easy to believe leadership is about fame, fortune, or philanthropy, but in truth leadership is about using your tools to change the lives of people you meet every day.

Too many leaders—established and emerging—believe their impact must be large and immediate. But what if you, like Maggie, were meant to maximize your leadership by lifting up the next generation of leaders? I believe men and women with tremendous influence share two common commitments: they serve and love people just as they are, but they also simultaneously encourage those same people to grow toward a future they didn't previously visualize.

ALWAYS FORWARD

- Who has positively impacted your life in unselfish ways that have propelled you forward? Who is doing this for you today?
- How can you use the lessons in your life to impact and serve others?
- It's the day of your funeral. Who do you hope will gather to celebrate your life? What stories do you want them to tell about you? What will you do today to make that happen?

YOUR UNIQUE JOURNEY

You might wish to apply my Mr. Countryman lesson in your life, or perhaps your unique journey involves a different, more valuable lesson for you today. If it helps, use pages 201–8 to remember instructive stories and experiences.

6

"I Know You Can"

HELPING OTHERS SEE THEIR FUTURE

I believe in the power one person has to change
the life of another.

Ron Kitchens

Congratulations, you are caller number thirteen, and you'll be joining us for our annual bus trip to see the Kansas City Royals!"

I was thrilled to hear these words over the phone. I was twelve, and I'd never seen a major league baseball game. I had no idea what to expect nor what impact this game would have on my life.

The big day came, and the three-hour bus ride was another first—my first time riding a bus by myself. When I finally arrived at the stadium, the sky was a vibrant blue and the grass was so green it was glowing. I noticed a group of other kids standing against the field's low fence. I walked down the stadium's steep steps and realized that they were trying to get autographs from the team on the other side of the fence. I didn't have a pen or anything for the players to sign, but I joined the small crowd. After a few minutes an older gentleman on the players' side walked up and started talking to the kids one by one. He asked each his or her name and age and what they wanted to be when they grew up.

Then he came to me. I quickly answered that someday I would like to work there in the stadium. I have no idea why I said that. I was overwhelmed and excited by the amazing, vibrant stadium.

The man's reply took me entirely by surprise. "Work here? Why not just own the place?"

I objected that I could never own the Royals. I rambled on about how I had had to win a ticket even to get there, and that I hadn't eaten because I didn't know what to do when the bus stopped at a cafeteria. I told him my dad died, and we were too poor to own things.

After a few more rapid sentences he stopped me and asked me to wait in the second row of seats. I instinctively assumed I was in trouble. They'd discovered I didn't belong there. I bet myself he was going to call security and have me thrown out. But the man was simply walking to a gate where he could exit the field and come sit next to me in the stands. Once he had, he said, "You really *could* own this place someday. Not long ago I was no richer than you, and now I own this team. If I can do it, you can too." He then shared with me his story of a life of tough breaks and countless failures. But he also showed me there was always a path forward. He told me how much he loved having people in the stadium.

The man was Ewing Kauffman, owner of the Kansas City Royals. Kauffman called down to pitcher Dennis Leonard and asked him to sign a ball. Leonard tossed the ball to Kauffman, who handed it to me. He then stood, thanked me for coming, and said, "Believe in yourself, or no one else will."

I still have that baseball, signed by Dennis Leonard. But more important, that marked the first time I remember a stranger ever trying to inspire me and lift my aspirations. It meant so much to have someone simply sit down and share time with me, even only a few fleeting minutes. It would have been just as easy for the team owner to keep moving down the row of kids and pass up that chance to impact my life. But Ewing Kauffman was an amazing man who made a conscious decision to invest in me that day. Incidentally, Kauffman left his life's fortune to the people of Kansas City. He really did believe in people.

● ● ●

Fast-forward six years. I was a high school senior, sauntering down the halls toward the counselor's office. I would be graduating soon, and the guidance counselor had summoned me for the all-important "next step" discussion. When I entered the office, I saw Carole Collins—my best friend's mother—sitting across from the counselor. She had always been like a second mom to me, but I thought it was odd that the guidance counselor had called her instead of my mom. I can only assume she believed Carole would have greater influence in reinforcing the message she was about to send me.

Before I could ask any questions, the counselor said coldly to Carole, "I have asked you here because Ron is clearly making a mistake. Based on his academic record, he should *not* go to college. He will be wasting his time and money." She explained that I did not have a future in postsecondary education. She never spoke to me or thought to ask what I wanted for my future. She never even glanced in my direction or acknowledged my presence.

Her words cut me to the bone. Hot humiliation burned from my heart to my head. I felt betrayed and victimized by this woman whose job it was to advocate for my interests.

Finally the counselor turned to me. "And my suggestion for you, young man, is that you look into becoming a furniture mover. I think that would be a suitable future for you."

Silence. I heard the buzzing fluorescent lights overhead. To this day, every time I hear that buzz, it takes me back to that chair and the crushing shame I felt.

Carole—a well-educated, wealthy, kind woman, whose husband was on the school board—leaned angrily forward in her chair. She uttered words that spoke to my soul, setting expectations that still propel me today. "You don't know what you're talking about! You don't have any idea who he is! You have no idea what he's going to achieve. I can't believe the evil you have done here today."

With one swift move Carole grabbed me by the arm and led me straight out to her car. After I'd pulled my leaden body into the passenger seat, I exploded into tears. I was utterly devastated.

Carole gently put my head on her lap, rubbed my back, and said, "It's okay. She doesn't know you. She doesn't know what you're going to achieve. You will achieve great things in your life. I believe in you." She just kept repeating over and over, "I believe in you. I believe in you. I believe in you."

Carole's mentoring and steadfast belief in my future were the only things that sustained me through that perilous time. It would take me twice as long as most to get through college. I worked hard and had plenty of reasons to quit school early, but I could not let Carole down. She had defended me when I was vulnerable and believed in me when I had no hope of my own.

People often do not consider their words or the impact they could have on others. A simple sit-down with a kid before a baseball game may do more to boost his or her confidence than you can imagine. Conversely, the careless words of a guidance counselor, even though they may contain some truths, could have irreparably changed my life's trajectory if Carole had not rescued me.

Nineteenth-century writer Walt Whitman struggled for years to attract anyone's interest in his poetry. He became very discouraged. But then he received a note: "Dear sir, I am not blind to the worth of the wonderful gift of *Leaves of Grass*. I find it the most extraordinary piece of wit and wisdom that America has yet contributed. . . . I greet you at the beginning of a great career."[1]

It was signed by Ralph Waldo Emerson. I can't help wondering what might have happened to Whitman had Emerson not invested in him with those kind words. Whitman must have breathed in the encouragement, finding inspiration to keep writing.

You don't have to be a professional writer like Emerson to make a difference in someone's life. Just taking the time to write a note of encouragement can be a meaningful investment in a person. Look for opportunities to pay people meaningful compliments. Tell them about strengths and positive traits you see in them. You never know when your affirmation might help at a key turning point.

ALWAYS FORWARD

- When has someone encouraged you with fresh vision for your future? What did they see in you? How did their belief in you impact you? In what ways are you still faithful to their vision?
- In whom might you inspire fresh confidence this week? How might you help them see their future with new hope?
- How would your relationships, personal and professional, change if you focused on what you can give instead of what you can get?

YOUR UNIQUE JOURNEY

You are welcome to apply my Ewing Kauffman lesson in your life, or maybe your story wants to teach you something more important for this moment. On pages 201–8 I've provided a list of categories and prompts that might help you brainstorm and remember instructive stories and experiences.

7

Lagniappe

A LITTLE SOMETHING EXTRA

How far that little candle throws its beams! So shines a good deed in a naughty world.

William Shakespeare

We at Southwest Michigan First look for team members who are amazing at what they do. We are also looking for people who will go just a little further than the competition. They make a habit of adding that something extra that we call "lagniappe" (pronounced *lan-yap*)—a Creole term. An example of lagniappe is when you order a bowl of ice cream and also receive whipped cream on top. Or that thirteenth donut thrown in when you buy a dozen. It strikes me that these days we all could use a little lagniappe in our lives.

I am reminded of an anniversary that my wife, Lyn, and I spent in New Orleans. I'm a child of the South, and specifically the Mississippi River, so New Orleans has a special place in my heart. And stomach. To celebrate this special occasion we selected Commander's Palace, one of the nation's great restaurants. We were seated on time and served a great meal by attentive servers who were knowledgeable about the food and wine. But that wasn't lagniappe.

The lagniappe came when head chef Jamie Shannon, the guy who succeeded Emeril Lagasse, came out from the kitchen with the owner, Ella Brennan, and thanked us for selecting them for such a special occasion. They then presented us with a signed, inscribed menu of the evening. That's lagniappe. I've eaten a lot of great meals at famous restaurants, but I will always remember this one because of that something special.

As another example, on a cold, wet evening this past winter my wife and I went to the Radisson Plaza Hotel in downtown Kalamazoo—home of one of our favorite restaurants. We left the car with valet parking and went in to dinner.

Following our great meal we retraced our steps, expecting to wait in the foyer while our car was retrieved. Lo and behold, it was already there waiting on us, with the heater running. I asked the valet how he knew we were coming, and he explained that our server saw the valet ticket in my pocket. When she presented our bill, she called to let them know we were almost ready. Lagniappe.

But that's not the end. I found that the driver's heated seat had also been turned on. It occurred to me that the valet might have done this for his own comfort, but Lyn discovered that the passenger seat had also been turned on.

Do you think that made my wife feel special? Absolutely. This was a classic lagniappe experience.

The Southwest Michigan First team is well versed in lagniappe experiences that give our clients and guests the best experience with us. We always strive for flawless event execution, which has come to be expected. At the conclusion of one event, rain was pouring down. Every available team member escorted guests to their cars under huge umbrellas. You can imagine the feedback that generated. What is more, as team members provided each attendee with this personal touch, we also listened carefully to their comments. This proved invaluable for our future planning and service.

Going that extra mile for your clients, guests, and team makes you a better leader; it requires you to think deeper for ideas that go further than expected. It forces you to consider what will make someone say "Wow!" That little something extra can be added anywhere—not just at events but in other ways too, such as in meetings or product delivery. Going above and beyond will ensure you stand out among the crowd.

The best marketing is word of mouth, and lagniappe experiences guarantee people will talk about your organization.

ALWAYS FORWARD

- When has someone added that something extra to your experience?
- Where can you add lagniappe in your services to others?

YOUR UNIQUE JOURNEY

You are welcome to apply my lagniappe lesson in your life, or maybe your story wants to teach you something more important for this moment. On pages 201–8 I've provided a list of categories and prompts that might help you brainstorm and remember instructive stories and experiences.

8

"Let Me Predict Your Future"

HARD TRUTH, SPOKEN IN LOVE

The future belongs to those who believe in the beauty of their dreams.

Eleanor Roosevelt

Let me predict your future: you are going to drop out of college in a semester or two. Not because you're not smart enough but because of a flat tire. The truth is, you don't have enough margin in your life. Something as small as a flat tire will force you to borrow money, causing you to take fewer classes at school so you can work more and pay your debt. Maybe you will even take a semester off to get caught up. Within a year or so you're going to get some girl pregnant and abandon your dream of escaping poverty. A few years later you will be the most popular guy on the assembly line at the ceiling fan factory on the edge of town."

Ouch. I was nineteen when I heard these words, and three decades later they still make me cringe. This hard truth came from a businessman who would go on to be my mentor and lifelong friend, and someone who would introduce me to four other men who would also change my life. His words were as painful as any I have heard, but they were also, without a doubt, some of the most formative of my life.

Many leaders get derailed because they have no one honest enough to help redirect their lives. We live in a society that speaks the language of participation trophies and protecting self-esteem. We often fail to recognize our need for a backup plan in case things go awry, nor do we have mentors to guide us. We become victims of change, not agents of change. Great leaders are marked by an openness to hearing hard truths and a willingness to act upon them thoughtfully.

After my guidance counselor tried to condemn me to a life of moving furniture, I became determined to prove her wrong. More than that, I resolved to prove Carole right for believing in me and my future. I would go to college. I had no passion for a specific major or career—I just knew I needed a diploma. Since I first learned to read in second grade, I'd heard Mrs. Names's voice in the back of my head, telling me college would be my future. I knew college equaled a good job, and people with careers enjoyed stability and pride. And that was what I wanted more than anything. I was determined that my family would never depend on a government check arriving on the third of every month; our experience would be different from mine as a child after my father's death.

I certainly didn't want to hear the truth from my mentor, that the traditional route to a diploma was not in the cards for me. But I knew his harsh prediction was meant to wake me up. This businessman knew I could succeed but also knew I had no financial margin—the hallmark of the working poor. So I would need to plot an unorthodox path to my degree in order to maneuver around inevitable challenges.

As predicted, my car broke down soon after. But it wasn't just the tires that failed; I had to buy a different car, loading my shoulders with even more debt. I would call this the fulfillment of the businessman's grim prediction, except that, thankfully, God put people in my life to lift me up when I needed them most.

● ● ●

Growing up in a small town was an incredible blessing. There weren't the same job opportunities offered in a big city, but in my case it allowed me to connect with experienced, successful mentors. Our community gave me access to outstanding people who would shape the rest of my life and who felt an obligation to care for their neighbors. In the turmoil of my late teens and early twenties, four men, all old enough to be my father or grandfather—a banker, a judge, an entrepreneur, and a merchant—made sure I found a successful path. Each on his own encouraged me to go into business while I attended college part-time.

Business was not a new concept for me; I was an entrepreneur before I knew what that word meant. I was a hustler, stopping each morning before elementary school to buy bubble gum to sell to my classmates, breeding rabbits to sell at Easter, and buying garage sale items to resell at swap meets. But the impact these four men would make went beyond transactions. They saw more in me than I would ever have seen on my own.

The merchant taught me to focus on caring for people first. He told me that, as long as I did that, the profits would follow.

The judge came by weekly to talk about business growth, asking me whom I'd met that week—people with whom I could potentially do business. He also offered to introduce me to people. He had been a successful attorney, and as an elected judge he knew well the value of relationships and the importance of nurturing and sharing them. Even though he knew I was working over eighty hours per week, he encouraged me to volunteer in the community. "You know," he said, "the time you spend volunteering is not just to be charitable. It's about growing a community so you can grow your business." He introduced me to the concept of enlightened self-interest.

The entrepreneur was a godsend. He showed me how to buy freight salvage—bulk goods with one or two damaged items—and resell the remainder at dramatic discounts. This increased my company profits and created surprising value for my customers. It was the merchant who ensured that I understood the importance of education and required that, if I wanted his help, I had to stay in college, taking at least one class a semester.

The banker taught me about money—how to know if I was making a profit, how to save for and pay taxes, how to balance cash flow, how to hire, and the difference between spending and investing. He was there to support my sometimes-crazy entrepreneurial startups—importing and exporting rugby equipment, buying vintage gas station signs for collectors, and repackaging fishing lures. Today these would be called "side hustles," but to me they were another way to create businesses and jobs for my community.

The banker completely changed the direction of my life in yet another way. I had just paid off a bank loan and was joyously celebrating with him. I was telling him how I could grow by hiring more people. He replied, "You care more about jobs than making a profit."

I'd never heard it put that way, and something clicked in my mind: that was exactly what I wanted. Even if I were to lift myself out of poverty, it didn't mean that much unless I could do the same for others. I exclaimed, "You finally get me!"

"I didn't mean that as a compliment," he said. "One of these days the economy will soften, or a project will fail, and you are going to lose everything. Everyone will lose their jobs. We have to find you a different path."

That next path had already revealed itself; I just didn't know it. There are advantages to being young, excited, and naïve; for me they were fearlessness and a keen sense of justice. Looking at my community, I wanted to find a way to have the greatest positive impact. I was frustrated about our local economy and that none of my friends who had left town for college would come home after graduation—there were no jobs. Once I complained about this problem to one of my mentors, the businessman who first told me my future. His advice was, "Why are you waiting? You have what it takes to do something about it!" His words emboldened me to run for city council in Ozark, Missouri, and I won.

Truth is, I won three city council elections in landslides. Okay, no one ever ran against me, but hey, a win is a win! My fellow council members, all old enough to be my parents or grandparents, elected me leader of the council—the mayor pro tem—on three separate occasions. Not bad for a twenty-one-year-old.

My city council tenure established a new vision for my life: to bring together the power of business, government, and philanthropy to change the lives of as many people as possible. This is a concept we now call "community capitalism" at Southwest Michigan First. While I love business, I love much more the impact it has on others.

I realized that, if I were ever going to be successful in the way I wanted, a traditional business would not help me get there. I needed a mission-driven enterprise. Keep in mind that this was before the days of Toms Shoes or Warby Parker, when business for the purpose of social impact became mainstream.

● ● ●

I value most those who can be honest with me and who care about my interests enough to have crucial, sometimes painful, conversations. But no matter how difficult the topic, discussions with the best mentors are tempered with compassion. The sage advice I received has served not only me but also the thousands of companies with whom I've consulted and tens of thousands of people who have gained jobs as a result. Some people don't see the value of mentors, even though all have had them. I ask leaders to name three people who changed their lives; they usually identify a teacher, a coach, and a boss. We've all had people in our lives who've introduced us to people, places, and ideas that have changed us forever.

Great leaders use their strengths and honesty for focused leadership and by it create a wake of positive impact behind them. This is like freeride wakeboarding: if your boat generates enough wake, you can surf behind the boat without a rope. In the same way, leaders who create a wake that's wide and strong enough provide their team opportunities to go forward and pursue greatness. Ultimately they'll shoot out of that wake with enough speed to lead on their own.

This is an integral part of our strategy at Southwest Michigan First. We want to put people in positions where they can grow their own leadership. In some cases it means starting new companies under the Southwest Michigan First umbrella. These include companies such as Consultant Connect, which provides economic development consulting to agencies throughout North America, or Catalyst University, which provides leadership and organizational training to more than three thousand leaders annually.

I was blessed to have strong relationships with my mentors early in my career, a blessing that continues today. When you need specific advice, a coach can be a powerful solution. Great organizations in America have utilized business consultants since the 1920s, but the high cost has traditionally denied them to all but the largest corporations. However, in the past decade we've seen an explosion of expertise available for every budget in the areas of business, church, and individual leadership. Emerging leaders are no longer stifled by lack of mentors.

● ● ●

One of my favorite leaders in history is Sacagawea, the Lemhi Shoshone woman who guided Lewis and Clark from Missouri to the Pacific Ocean. She was a sixteen-year-old pregnant slave whose "husband" conscripted her into Lewis and Clark's mission. During her travels west she had her baby and negotiated with tribes for food and horses when stores became so low they had to eat tallow candles. Lewis and Clark had access to all of the resources the nation could muster, but could not succeed without the guidance and mentoring of a girl with a baby on her back.

I'm a terrible golfer. I have never enjoyed a day on the golf course, but it's not for lack of trying. I own the right clubs, clothes, and shoes. But I'm still an awful golfer. And yet earlier in my career I was expected to understand at least the basics of the game to find any success in business. So I hired a coach, hoping, with his help, at least not to embarrass myself.

No one ever questioned that it made sense for me to hire a golf coach. But if I reveal that for the past twenty years I've always had a management coach, many people immediately believe I am being punished, or perhaps I'm as deficient at managing as I am with a nine iron. However, unlike golf, leadership happens to be a personal strength of mine. But I want to be better. I acknowledge that, no matter how good I am at something, there is always room for improvement.

Whenever I talk to emerging leaders about their need for coaching and guidance, they tend to become embarrassed or assume I'm nicely telling them they don't have what it takes to succeed. I see in their eyes some of the pain that I felt in the high school counselor's office—being told I was a failure before I ever started. To me this notion is utterly ridiculous. I eventually gave up trying to learn golf, because for me it wasn't worth the time. I knew that, no matter how much I trained, I would never really enjoy it. But other things are worth the energy! Leadership is an area in which I've always excelled, making it well worth a lifetime of effort to cultivate.

Just as an athlete needs a strength and conditioning coach, I need somebody who gets up every day to keep me accountable to my goals and make sure I'm reading the right books, listening to the top podcasts, and following the best blogs to fill the gaps in my knowledge and capacity.

ALWAYS FORWARD

- When has a hard truth, spoken in love, proven helpful to you?
- Imagine, without any limitations, who you would choose as a mentor. What lessons do you want to learn from them? From their mentoring, what results would you expect in your life, leadership, and organization? What's holding you back from learning from them in person, or via video, writings, or podcasts?
- What three areas in your leadership would be accelerated by coaching?

YOUR UNIQUE JOURNEY

My lesson about mentors might be just what you need in your life and leadership. But consider also whether your unique life experience offers something even more valuable. Pages 201–8 might help you find what your story is trying to teach you now.

9

"That's Not Our Plan"

STAYING TRUE TO YOUR DREAMS

A dream is something you really want to do, but
a calling is something you have to do.

John Maxwell

I am doing a great work and I cannot come down." This
message greets me every morning at six. Given the never-
ending onslaught of tweets, emails, and phone calls, I must
remain intentional about my focus, and this short statement
reminds me that impactful leaders are focused leaders.

This quote, from Nehemiah 6:3, dates to 445 BC and
was spoken by a Jewish slave named Nehemiah. He was
the trusted cupbearer and food taster for King Artaxerxes I
of Persia, in the region of modern-day Iran. Over time
Nehemiah had heard continued rumors that Jerusalem was
being attacked by savage warlords who were enslaving the

people and stealing with impunity. Even though he'd never visited Jerusalem, Nehemiah was overwhelmed by a calling to save the city of his ancestors. One day he finally asked the king if he could go and help his people. Artaxerxes told Nehemiah he would give him whatever resources he needed to rebuild the wall protecting the city, but Nehemiah must promise to return. Talk about trust from your boss. In essence the king said, "If it's important to you, it's important to me."

As you would expect, not everyone near Jerusalem was happy that Nehemiah had shown up with his leadership and supplies. Those who benefited from Jerusalem's insecurity hated losing their freedom to pillage. Not surprising. Those with the most to gain from the status quo always resist change.

As Nehemiah began his work, Jerusalem's non-Jewish neighbors grew angry. They started stealing Nehemiah's resources to inhibit his work. Enemy leaders and influencers tried to get Nehemiah to come down from the wall to meet; they tried flattery, fear, and even bribes. They sent troops to attack him and his workers. They spread rumors that his true purpose was to make himself king and rebel against Persia. Even people he thought were his friends were hired to turn on him, but their efforts could not stop Nehemiah from fulfilling his calling. And you thought social media trolls were bad.

Status quo is one of the most dangerous traps for individuals, groups, or organizations. At best status quo ensures mediocrity. At worst it imprisons people in the belief that risks related to change are greater than risks from staying the same.

When my wife, Lyn, and I first began dating, she worked at a children's home for abused and neglected young women and girls. As our relationship developed, I grew to love Lyn's commitment to helping those women see a different future for themselves. Her battle was not about mending these young ladies' physical injuries but convincing them they deserved better, even if they couldn't define it. They suspected change and sought security in the status quo of their lives, even if it was, in truth, a danger to them.

Nehemiah knew that survival required change. His response to the many attacks was simple yet so powerful that I, 2,500 years later, still look to his statement to guide my life and leadership. Each time he was approached, Nehemiah responded the same way: "I am doing a great work and I cannot come down."

On October 2, 445 BC, fifty-two days after starting his project, Nehemiah finished the wall around Jerusalem. He provided safety and security to people who had never known they could achieve it. He saved an entire region and changed the course of history, all because he refused to be distracted.

As men and women driven to change the future, we too must stay on our ladders, building our walls. We too are called to use the bricks and mortar we've been given to build the walls of our futures. We need to make an unshakable commitment to our vision and to lead *big*. We must ignore distractions that would derail us from our work, remembering Nehemiah's words: "I am doing a great work and I cannot come down."

● ● ●

If your dream is easily attainable, it's not big enough. That is not meant to diminish your passion but to inspire it. A dream should be kind of scary—at first you should not know exactly how you're going to achieve it. Big, impossible dreams do come true, but they should not be mere fantasies. Great leaders also recognize that the journey is part of the dream; rarely does someone achieve their goal without enjoying the ride along the way.

That's why it's essential to always be thinking about the next step you should take to achieve your dream. Please never settle. It's easy to become comfortable along the way. When your vision seems far away, you might be tempted to decide to stop sacrificing your comforts in pursuit of something uncertain.

Even worse, perhaps you've achieved your dream and have no idea what to strive for next. I see many leaders fall off the leadership path because they reach their objectives and don't know how to expand and dream bigger. One of our challenges as leaders is to ask ourselves constantly, *What is my next dream? And what is my plan to get there?*

At Southwest Michigan First we coach our teammates and coworkers to dream big dreams but also to evaluate what their goals indicate about their leadership. If someone tells me their dream is to become a US president, I always ask why. In the next forty years we will have only five to ten presidents from among more than three hundred million people living in the United States. Many dreams, though technically achievable, are masks hiding deeper desires. Your earnest desire may be to have influence. Perhaps your passion is to end childhood poverty. It's an oversimplification to believe that, if you were president, you could singlehandedly solve child poverty or whatever issue is important to you.

My question back is always, "Who else could solve this problem?" Frankly, if your zeal is around one specific issue, you can have larger impact working at a smaller, more local level than you ever could as president. I've often said I want to be a United States ambassador after my career. Why? I want to represent the United States because I think it truly is the best country in the world. But realistically I could do that in many other ways. I could represent my country as the president of a major foundation or by writing a book that is distributed globally. I dream of that kind of impact, not the specific job of ambassador. We leaders gravitate toward what is comfortable, definable, or expected, but that doesn't necessarily mean it's our actual dream.

●　●　●

Graduating from college for me was an eight-year process, but it was a commitment I made to my mentors, my soon-to-be wife, and myself. My plan was not just to graduate but to focus my life on growing jobs.

When I was one semester away from graduating, my plans were challenged. I was asked to meet with a group of dentists. They were starting a new dental insurance program and wanted me to be president of their company. My ego was both flattered and thrilled that these men would seek me out. From a financial standpoint this was an incredible opportunity, and my salary would start immediately. This job would change everything. Lyn and I would be able to marry immediately, start a family, and buy a home in a great neighborhood. No longer would we have to sell our blood at the local plasma center to afford extras. We would finally even be able to purchase more than a week's worth of toilet paper at a time. The position would allow us to achieve the American Dream overnight.

When I saw Lyn, my first words were, "We have hit the jackpot! You can have any house you want. They want me as the president of the company!"

Her response was both simple and catalytic: "That sounds great, but that's not our plan."

She continued, "Our plan was for you to graduate from college, and then you were going to work in economic development. Now, we can change the plan, but we need to talk about it first—not about money, not about the position, but about what happens to our plan. You promised my parents you were going to graduate from college. That was part of the agreement for us getting married. We can change that, but just because you got this offer doesn't mean we should automatically abandon the course of our lives and our dreams."

Lyn would have loved a jump start on our life together, but she was more committed to living our authentic, God-granted purpose.

That was one of the hardest decisions I've ever had to make. I knew taking this opportunity would change my life, that overnight I would have prestige, social presence, and money. But at what cost? And would the change be for the better?

While I didn't yet know the story of Nehemiah, this was the start of my Nehemiah journey. If it were only me, I would have come down off the wall and set aside my plan. I would have quit school one semester short, disappointed those who had supported and mentored me, and, most significantly, squandered the gifts of passion and talent God had given me.

I think too many times we leaders are looking for a magic bullet, a miracle job offer, or a winning lottery ticket. I'm not saying that if you work hard and an opportunity comes your way, you should not take it just because it came as a surprise. But sometimes you will face decisions that will test your foundations.

Lyn's comments, spoken with love, kept me on my wall, honoring my commitments. Her words lifted me up and eventually allowed me the incredible impact and influence of which I always dreamed. Insurance is a great business, and those dentists were outstanding people, but that was not my Jerusalem. My dream was never to run an insurance company, and it certainly was not to merely make money.

As leaders, we have to understand what is fundamental to our plans. Sometimes that means setting aside our short-term desires so we can achieve our life's purpose. And we need people to hold us accountable to our commitments and keep us from getting lost, becoming distracted, or chasing money, prestige, or someone else's vision for us.

ALWAYS FORWARD

- What is your Jerusalem wall? What dream does wisdom require you to dismiss and allow others to complete?
- What distractions are keeping you from achieving what you were created for?

- Who is holding you accountable to staying focused on your mission and dreams?

YOUR UNIQUE JOURNEY

You're welcome to apply my Nehemiah lesson, or perhaps a different lesson from your experience is what you need right now. Consider using pages 201–8 to help find it.

10

The Four Horses

UNDERSTANDING THE RACE YOU WERE
CREATED TO RUN

If you spend your life trying to be good at everything, you will never be great at anything.

Tom Rath

At twelve I got my first real job, working as a stable hand
in a horse barn, which is a polite way of saying I made a
dollar fifty per hour to shovel horse manure and wash sweaty
horses. And though it wasn't glamorous, it was one of the
formative experiences of my life.

During the twenty hours each week I spent in the barn I
was able to learn many life lessons. This instilled in me the
values of keeping my word and being punctual. I learned that
those in my care always come before me and that people who
were cruel to animals are never to be trusted. I still carry these

principles with me, but the most profound lesson I learned in the horse stalls was that, like a person, a successful horse must focus on the area of its greatest strength.

I discovered there are four kinds of horses:

1. *Thoroughbred horses* are born to run very fast over about a mile. They are beautiful, high-strung, and creatively named. But they're not going to do any real work. If you put a thoroughbred in a harness to plow, you'll find it's not physically up to the task. They are simply not built for work.

2. *Quarter horses* are as American as cowboys and cattle drives. Watching a rider and quarter horse work together to herd cattle is almost a spiritual experience. I love these horses. They're smart and thrive working in tandem with a rider. But if you put a quarter horse in a thoroughbred race, it doesn't stand a chance of keeping up; the thoroughbreds will outrun the quarter horse every time.

3. *Plow horses* are the proverbial workhorse. They plow fields, harvest crops, and have even been mythologized by a certain beer company, pulling their distinctive wagon. Years ago plow horses hauled early fire equipment and built our economy. They're designed for their day-after-day stamina and ability to work hard, but don't ask them to run races or herd cattle.

4. *Show horses* are beautiful both visually and athletically. They are meant solely to look fine and perform, much like a classical dancer. The barn where I worked specialized in Tennessee Walking Horses that wore elevated

shoes. This hoofwear gave them an exaggerated trot, and they served no other purpose than to entertain and win prizes. Show horses can neither plow, run long distances, nor herd cattle, but they are beautiful to watch.

Comparing the four horses reminds me of a quote by an unknown author (which is often misattributed to Albert Einstein): "Everybody is a genius. But if you judge a fish by its ability to climb a tree, it will live its whole life believing that it is a failure." I believe every person has a seed of greatness inside; they have unique talents and strengths imbued by our Creator. It's our responsibility as leaders to help those we lead to understand their abilities and strengths and, like horses, to optimally operate within their areas of gifting and excellence.

That said, there will be times when, due to pure necessity, we are forced to adapt and work outside the areas that give us energy. I have a picture in my home office of Babe Ruth and Lou Gehrig, taken in October 1928, shortly after the New York Yankees swept the St. Louis Cardinals in the World Series. Ruth and Gehrig were on top of the world that day. They remain the two most famous baseball players of their time, possibly ever. And yet in that photo they look rather ridiculous. The duo looks slightly uncomfortable, dressed in cowboy hats, chaps, and spurs to promote Madison Square Garden's World Series Rodeo.

I learned more about the history of that photo, and it became clear that neither player really wanted to be in the rodeo promotion business. But the task was a job requirement, so of course they did it. I treasure this picture as a reminder that, regardless of our positions or professions or levels of success, sometimes we all must pay a price to do what we love.

I think there is a perception, especially among emerging leaders, that once you arrive at a certain level of leadership or success, you will no longer have to do anything you don't want to do. This picture is proof that's not the case. On days when I'm unenthused about my schedule or spend hours on something outside my passion, I look at this photo and remember we all must occasionally put on our furry chaps and cowboy hats so we can do the work we love. Sometimes being forced to dress up like a rodeo clown is the price of being great. Or as my wife, Lyn, says, "It doesn't matter if you're a CEO; it's still your job to take out the trash."

We just need to make sure this task doesn't become continuous and dominate our existence. The majority of your job should be engaging and fulfilling. If you are a quarter horse, you should spend your career driving cattle and constantly finding ways to be the best at what you do. If you are not working in your strengths, you are working in your weaknesses. No one hired you for that. At Southwest Michigan First we take the time to stop and evaluate every forty days to make sure each team member is doing what he or she does best. This increases everyone's capacity and expands their ability to deliver on our commitment to be preeminent.

It's great working on a team where everyone is hired for and focused on their strengths, because it's like playing every game with an all-star team. You get to do life with the best of the best.

When hiring new employees, typical organizations focus on résumés, transcripts, references, and titles. Great organizations focus on selecting the best people based on talent, strengths, and fit. Southwest Michigan First's selection process is unique and requires the full commitment and intellectual and emotional ownership of all team members. Our process is purposefully long and requires a commitment from both the team and the applicant, but I believe the outcome is worth it.

The Process

We look at our work and its requirements like a big family-style offering of food. Once the meal is prepared, each dish must be selected and placed on an existing team member's plate. We know we need to hire a new member when the amount of food on someone's plate exceeds his or her appetite. We also hire if a team member, with permission, switches their food for something on other dishes. That leaves us with an unassigned plateful of food and a clear direction for someone new.

The Steps

1. A team member is assigned to lead the hiring process. This leader will not be the new person's supervisor and, in most cases, will not even work in the same area. This leader's role is concierge of the process; he or she serves as the new hire's best friend for their first ninety days of joining our team.
2. An agreement is reached on the need for and the role of the new position.
3. All team members are briefed on the position and a profile of the ideal candidate. They are asked to circulate the

opportunity through their personal and social networks. A local recruitment partner, WSI Talent, is brought on board to begin screening applicants as they are identified.

4. Management team members gather and evaluate applicants, and the perceived best candidates move forward for the talent evaluation survey by WSI. Candidates who meet our predetermined threshold for talent evaluation are given the Gallup StrengthsFinder evaluation, which is then reviewed by the management team leader in the candidate's area and the concierge team member. If approved, the candidate is scheduled for a management team fit interview, involving two members of the management team and one recently hired teammate.

The process continues until a minimum of three candidates are identified to move forward to the team fit process. One of these candidates must be a minority candidate—that is, they either fit the traditional definition of "minority candidate" or they differ from the person who fit that role in the past.

5. Next, the team fit interviews take place. These are not about résumé, talents, or strengths, as those have already been verified. This is a time for interviewers to ask themselves:

   a. Do I want to spend half of my waking hours with this person?
   b. Do I believe this person has the "right stuff" to lead at the pace of our team?
   c. Am I willing to tell our CEO and board, "I believe this person has what it takes to succeed on our team,

85

and I understand their success or failure is a direct reflection of my leadership and ability"?

Every member of the team meets with candidates in groups no larger than six in settings such as a meal, boardroom, or social context. They're encouraged to consider independently the candidate's fit. Once the team fit interview is complete, each interviewer sends a message stating their support or reservations to the concierge team member.

6. Any candidate who gains the full support of the team moves forward to an interview with the CEO, where a candidate may be offered employment.

Talent is the differentiator for which we hire. Your marketing and technology can be incredible, but talent is what differentiates between average and incredible. But no matter how amazing they are, people still need mentoring and feedback.

The Cultivation

For thousands of years, forty days has been the measure of a recognized rhythm. It contrasts with the standard monthly rhythm for working around the holiday seasons and popular summer vacation times. Consider the historic forty-day periods of rain, fasting, taunting by Goliath before he meets David, and many other mentions in the Bible. Forty days creates an impactful rhythm.

At Southwest Michigan First each person designs a customized report, which we call a 4:40, in which they record their goals for the year (or longer) as well as important areas

86

for the next forty days' focus in order to accomplish those goals. This opens a dialogue to discuss obstacles impeding those goals, but these regular check-ins are not exclusively about performance. We encourage team members to ask their mentor partners for additional resources or support. We ask questions like, What is your plan for your career, and how do I help with that? And most important, What do you need to succeed?

This opens an opportunity for team members to ask for small things: "I need a new laptop. Mine keeps crashing, and I can't use the program that would really help because the computer won't support it." Team members can also bring up larger concerns: "I feel a need to earn a master's degree," for example, or "I want to become certified in economic development or event management." I can support them, and we can start a plan to invest in their success.

I encourage you to challenge the traditional practice of annual reviews without intermediate check-ins. Whether you adopt our 4:40 system (see appendix A for more information) or develop a strategy of your own, consider if your system is actually providing you with anything valuable. Great organizations are doing regular, real-time checkups. They don't wait a year to beat somebody up merely because that's the way business has always been done.

It's vital that expectations are clear and that everyone in an organization knows where they stand. And it is equally important that each team member be affirmed, supported, and given necessary resources. I think our 4:40 innovation is one of the reasons Southwest Michigan First has seen the success we've enjoyed. It helps us hold true to our philosophy that each person is the CEO of their own responsibility. It also ensures that goals are defined, resources are provided, and strategies toward success are developed collaboratively.

Google has a system similar to our 4:40s. They call their system OKR (objectives and key results). They focus on setting, measuring, tracking, and using solid data. If the world's most valuable company and a company named the Best Small Business in America both value the same type of system, I bet it's right for your organization too.

● ● ●

I'm regularly asked, "If you focus so much on building talented people to be incredible, aren't you afraid they'll leave?" My simple answer is no. If I truly commit to my team and expect them to commit to each other, I'm responsible to ensure my people get their dream jobs. I work hard to ensure that dream job is with us, but if it's not, that doesn't diminish my responsibility to help them connect with it somewhere else. I've sometimes been concerned that I wouldn't offer opportunities big enough for a team member. But I consciously decide to pour into them and build amazing leaders, regardless of the long-term outcome.

Every headhunter in our industry knows they're encouraged to contact my team members directly. And my team members know that, if they're considering a new position, I want to be a reference for them. I want to be quoted in the press release about how lucky the new organization is to have them. I want to help them negotiate their deals. I'm proud to have had the opportunity to work with nine former team members who are now leading their own organizations. If I had a little something to do with their success and increasing their impact on the world, I consider that one of my greatest achievements.

When we lose a great team member, we almost always find a replacement with strong potential who is already on our team.

And we are not alone. Nick Saban, University of Alabama's head football coach, famously invests in coworkers, even if they one day may become his competitors. At the start of the 2018 season, four of his former staff were coaching against him in the Southeast Conference.

ALWAYS FORWARD

- What type of horse are you? Ask three people you trust (not including your mom) how they would describe your talents and strengths.
- Where in your life are you "a fish trying to climb a tree"? How can you stop working in that area?
- If you were building the strongest team possible for your organization, what would be the attributes of each role?
- If you designed a regular monitoring and review process, what would it look like?

YOUR UNIQUE JOURNEY

You are welcome to apply my four horses lesson in your life, or maybe your story wants to teach you something more important for this moment. On pages 201–8 I've provided a list of categories and prompts that might help you brainstorm and remember instructive stories and experiences.

11

Great Teams

WHAT IT TAKES TO WIN

Talent is the product. With the right people, given
the correct incentives, encouraged and driven
to their highest individual accomplishments,
blended into a balanced and adaptive team, win-
nowed when they can't succeed, you will adapt
to competitive challenges. Talent is the product.

Jeff Angus

The longer I'm in leadership, the more I'm fascinated by
teams. In fact, I probably think and write about teams
more than anything else these days.

A few months ago I was reflecting on teams and came
across an interesting concept about cycling. In order to win
a big race like the Tour de France, the front rider—the one
who gets the biggest product endorsements and wears the
coveted yellow jersey—has to surround himself with a team

of other athletes who are equally as high-performing but who have different strengths and talents. This concept struck me as I watched the Tour de France earlier this summer and heard the commentators talking about the member of the leading team who carried water to keep his team hydrated. At first he sounded to me like a mere water boy, but I soon realized he had to be a world-class rider—good enough to lead a different team. But instead he chose a servant's role on a great team.

This reminded me of Southwest Michigan First's team and made me proud. On our business cards, website, and social media we always write our titles in lowercase letters, because titles don't really matter here. We use uppercase to write our organization name and our mission. Those are most important.

We have world-class riders on this team who come from other organizations where they've had bigger titles or more responsibilities but haven't had opportunities for real influence or impact. These leaders understand that not everyone can be known as the front rider. If the person carrying the water doesn't do his or her job and keep up with the pace of the rest, the team doesn't win. There may be smaller titles or less glamorous responsibilities, but a world-class team has no small roles.

We leaders have to remember to recognize the influence and impact of all team members. Not everyone was made to be or wants to be the lead rider or the hill climber. In our case not everyone wants to be out front selling our organization and our community. Not everyone has the skills to do the creative work that gets public accolades. But as my grandfather used to say to me when I was twenty-one and still impressed with myself after being elected to office, "If you don't do your job as mayor pro tem for two weeks and the guy who picks up the trash doesn't do his job for two weeks, who do you think people will notice first and care more about?" This always reminded me that even though I was elected to wear the leader's title, it was everyone's job to provide great service to our city's citizens.

To be part of a great team, we have to check our egos at the door. One season you might carry water and another season you might be the celebrity cyclist, but we all must be great at what we do in order to achieve success together. And don't think for one second that the guy carrying water for the number-one team in cycling doesn't go home and brag about his role.

• • •

I see in other organizations the toll that expediency can take. This is especially true in the hiring process. It's obvious when management lacks a thoughtful strategy—their team tends to look exactly like its leader. We tend to hire people we know, who have personalities similar to our own, and who've gone to the same schools. So we unintentionally end up with organizations whose members reflect the same gender, ethnicity, and background as the leader. Without strategies to ensure diversity we're never going to achieve it. Without meaning to, hiring committees can unconsciously act like a group of fourth-graders judging the new kid. At Southwest Michigan First and on all the teams I've led, we have intentionally aimed for diversity and inclusivity.

I often receive notes asking how I put together such a talented team, usually following an event or program we've led.

It's always a flattering question, and I'd love to take credit for our team's success, but it wouldn't be right. Our success largely goes back to the talents and work ethics of all individuals, but more important, it ties to the way they work together. My role—the role all leaders can play—is establishing measures and practices to hire the right blend of people.

Diversity is hugely important. There are usually two camps of people—those who love talking about diversity and those tired of hearing about it. When I say diversity, I don't just mean the obvious—race, gender, age, sexual orientation. Diversity is much bigger, although those categories matter.

The ages of Southwest Michigan First's team members range from Generation Z to Baby Boomers. We're a predominantly female-driven organization in an industry typically dominated by men. We include many ethnicities—Asian, African American, Hispanic, Native American, and Caucasian. And it didn't happen by accident. We insist that one of the final candidates for each new hire must be atypical or represent a minority group; they bring a unique element to the table, differing from the other candidates.

If you've heard of the Rooney Rule, you know that the National Football League gets the importance of this. Established in 2003, this rule requires a team hiring a head coach to include at least one diverse candidate in the mix. The NFL is usually looking to hire a coach based on previous experience; we, on the other hand, evaluate future potential, but the concept is the same. A great team requires constantly analyzing the team makeup to find the gaps, which are filled best by diverse members.

We hire based on talent. Gallup has identified thirty-four areas of strength that we measure, and we purposefully hire people who are hardwired for success in a few important areas. But we also seek team members who will bring something new to the table. Some may be surprised that most of us are not economic developers by trade. Some of our team members have served as yoga instructors, stay-at-home moms, legislative staffers, educators, and interior designers. And our educational backgrounds vary as much as our work experience.

Why does this matter? Every generation of leaders talks about how the world is becoming more connected and complicated. They're absolutely correct. Immediate access to information makes it harder to be a leader in a particular industry sector, because everyone has the same knowledge. The requirements for success are much higher. Just to meet average standards, today's leaders and team members have to be more gifted than in the past. So outstanding greatness requires members who can solve problems from multiple perspectives.

The United States today enjoys full employment, and unless some unforeseen disaster strikes, that will continue for the next decade as a wave of Baby Boomers starts to retire. The best leaders and organizations understand that all future success is predicated on its ability to find and nurture the most talented people. That requires being intentional about the process.

Too many people contend that the entire hiring process should be blind. To that I say, "Bologna!" It's just not true. The process should be intentionally unblinded. You have to use every available resource to find the very best, rather than merely assuming a help wanted ad on Facebook will reach billions of the most qualified people. Chances are they're not going to see it.

94

I think it's shortsighted to hire purely based on the information on a résumé. All you can tell from a résumé is whether a candidate worked in the right field or at the right organizations. They might have twenty years' experience, or they might have the same year of experience replicated twenty times over. Any other "information" gleaned from a résumé is meaningless advertising meant to appeal to your biases. It still influences many hiring decisions, but if a candidate seems likable or familiar to you, that doesn't make them the best candidate—or even a good candidate.

Great organizations remove their biases and preconceptions from the process. They go after the greatest possible mix of talented candidates, then narrow to a few elite finalists. Then each candidate rises or falls based on his or her fit, capacity to lead, and ability to engage with the rest of the team. This process helps you harvest the best of the best from a universe of applicants.

Diversity equals destiny.

ALWAYS FORWARD

- In what role are you serving, and how does it impact your organization's successes?
- Do you want to change roles now or in the future? How are you preparing for a change?
- How can you better support your team?
- What experiences in your past can help improve your hiring process?

- If your organization conformed to the highest expectations for staff makeup, capacity, and skills, what difference would that make?

YOUR UNIQUE JOURNEY

If my lesson about teams is right on target for you, run with it. If not, what other lesson might you draw from your unique life experience, perhaps using the prompts provided on pages 201–8?

12

Surround Yourself

WHO IS MAKING YOU BETTER?

The world will tell you that you do not measure up. You need someone to encourage you, to tell you that you do.

Paul Rasmussen

The people with whom you surround yourself in many ways forge who you are and determine where you go. Jim Rohn hit it dead on: "You are the average of the five people you spend the most time with."[1]

My grandfather, who went a long way in raising me, reminded me every time I walked out the door that "stupid sticks." He was telling me not to surround myself with people I knew were going to be bad influences.

In our leadership we need to avoid people who drag us off course or backward. Instead surround yourself with people you admire, who know what you don't, and who've experienced what you haven't.

According to Harvard research psychologist Dr. David McClelland, the people you spend the most time with determine 95 percent of your success or failure in life.[2] This is the kind of wisdom that can help you choose a valuable board of directors. We usually hear about boards for publicly traded companies or nonprofits. But consider their function: there are many stereotypes and misconceptions, but boards are really about accountability. It's their job to keep your leadership in line with your mission. They encourage leaders to apply best organizational practices and grow the organization in ways that magnify their available resources.

But great leaders also have *personal* boards of directors—sounding boards and accountability partners who provide honest feedback and have no entangling interests. They're motivated by their love, respect, and support for you as a leader.

My friend Bob Goff—an author, speaker, and agent of joy—shared about his personal board at Catalyst University, our annual leadership conference. He said that those surrounding him are "a group of people I feel God has dropped into my life, kind of like a cabinet. These people have their particular areas of wisdom and experience, and I use them to bounce ideas off of and get their input. The people help me do some dead reckoning in my life; I use their counsel as a fixed point in my life and take a bearing from it, drawing a line from them to me."

I have friends and business colleagues who regularly meet with their personal boards in a formalized process. Others seek informal feedback as needed. The most important thing for a leader is to have a solid group of trusted confidants to call upon to ask those crucial questions, knowing that they will give their honest opinions.

I speak with some members of my personal board regularly by phone, in person, or through email or texts. With some I communicate weekly, others every six months or so. I share my hopes, needs, and desires. I ask for honest assessment of my leadership and guidance for achieving my dreams. I can't describe how influential this has been in my life.

How do I choose my personal board of directors? I'm very intentional about it. It's wholly based on trust. Who can I trust with my vulnerabilities? As I mentioned in this book's opening, I trusted almost no one till I was forty. I lived in fear that people would discover I didn't go to the right schools and that my upbringing was so humble. I decided to surround myself with people I could trust to keep my deepest secret, who would embrace that aspect of my life and not judge me for it. It's also critical that these women and men have been successful in their own lives. That might seem obvious, but I often see the opposite in those influencing leaders. And I consider two qualifications to be absolute requirements: they must make me smarter, and they must be able to consider lots of solutions before fixating on one.

Several of my personal board members are voracious readers, always on the cutting edge of knowledge and applying it in practical work. I also have members who don't care one iota about business success—they only care about me and my happiness. They check in to ask, "How are you doing personally? Tell me what's going on with your family, your health, your spiritual life."

My personal board was small until I began to develop my new willingness to trust people. After that my list began to grow exponentially. Sometimes I've asked formally, "Hey, would you join me on this journey?" And with some I've never officially discussed their membership on my personal board of directors; we have an unspoken commitment to each other. Every year I review my list of confidants and decide whom to add and how often I should meet with each.

Leaders starting their first personal board often ask whom they should choose. Assuming a size of eight people, my rule of thumb is to make sure one's board includes at least four women, two Millennials, two Generation Xers, one social media guru, two industry leaders, one faith or social leader, one creative (an artist, writer, or musician, for example), two entrepreneurs, and one design expert.

● ● ●

If leadership is lonely, it's a self-inflicted loneliness. If you aren't surrounding yourself with people you can trust—who pour love, vision, and encouragement into you—then you're not leading to your fullest potential, and you're going to feel alone.

Now, this must be a two-way street. While others are serving you, you are also responsible to serve in similar roles for others. Many leaders can give me lists of influential people investing in them, but then I ask, "Now, who are you serving?" And I hear only crickets. Who can you serve, and how are you doing that? Don't wait to be asked; just start helping. You'll find that your abilities will rise to meet the needs of those you serve.

I'm fascinated by people's power to influence those around them—whether on leadership teams, among athletes, or between friends. We can propel each other to achieve together what the individual may never accomplish. One of history's great friendships was that between Henry Ford, Thomas Edison, and Harvey Firestone. Greenfield Village in Dearborn, Michigan, is the home of the Ford Motor Company and the Henry Ford Museum, which chronicles Ford's relationship with Edison and Firestone.

The three called themselves "vagabonds." These three titans spent nearly every summer together for decades, camping and communing with nature. And they invited along famous friends such as Charles Lindbergh, John Burroughs, and even a couple of presidents.

The relationship between the three went beyond simple social friendship; they shared genuine love and concern for each other and their enterprises. Ford's engine design propelled automobiles from battery to gasoline. Henry Ford later recounted when Edison had encouraged him, banging the table and exclaiming, "That's the thing! You have it! Your car is self-contained and carries its own power plant." Ford later wrote, "That bang on the table was worth worlds to me. No man up to then had given me any encouragement."[3]

These men poured into each other with powerful results, changing the world.

Personal boards can be virtuous circles in which members support and lift up each other. I remember as a child reading about Café Guerbois in late-1800s Paris, where now-great artists such as Édouard Manet, Edgar Degas, Claude Monet, Pierre-Auguste Renoir, and Paul Cezanne hung out together, critiqued each other's pieces, arranged to show the group's work, and, in dire situations, ensured that each had enough money to continue. A few years ago I attended a course in Paris about this group of men and their impact on each other. The art historians leading the program believed that, even though their artistic and personal styles were different, it was their proximity and commitment to each other that made each member extraordinary.

Today, the Café Guerbois is a group of shops, but I snuck in to get a cup of coffee to see if any of the collaborative magic remained there.

But what if you live in a small community and can't seem to find a group to inspire and support you? Ideally you build a peer group in your area or within a day's drive. Being *physically* in community is imperative. As I study successful people in any sector, invariably the elite find ways to hang out together in person. But if your travel budget or contacts don't allow this, then starting with an online group is an acceptable alternative. Yet you should always work toward the ideal of face-to-face collaboration.

Early in my career I found myself isolated. Two friends and I then formed a group called Engage and invited select people to come together at their expense for a few days to share best practices. I did this for ten years, and my only real cost was the time it took to organize the events. Three of my friends have recently moved to Nashville to jump-start their careers by immersing themselves in that city's creative culture. But if you can't move to a new city and can't find a group to join, I suggest you build your own.

It's easy to criticize acquaintances and celebrities who encounter disaster because of the unhealthy company they keep. But we should work harder to examine people who are thriving in their lives, asking, "Why are they doing so well?" We should ask about the environments they frequent and the people with whom they associate, and how both contribute to their success.

We leaders should also encourage our team members to put themselves in positive situations and surround themselves with wise people, as well as to avoid toxic situations and people. This is why we at Southwest Michigan First believe it's important for our people to serve on boards in the community and with organizations that make them better—rubbing elbows with other great leaders. This is why we do a lot of coleading and partnering with other leaders, locally and nationally, instead of doing everything in a silo.

I am fascinated by the dynamics of push and pull in the universe, as in Newton's third law of motion, which states that the force of one body on another is accompanied by an equal and opposite force.[4] If Newton had written a law on leadership, it might have read, "Your impact and influence will grow in direct proportion to the people who invest in you and those into whom you choose to pour."

ALWAYS FORWARD

- Which five to eight people would form your ideal personal board? Be realistic, choosing people to whom you have access.
- With whom are you choosing to spend your time and your life, and how are they currently making you better? How can you increase that time or maximize its benefit?

- Whose "stupid" is sticking to you and bringing your life's trajectory down? What will you do to correct this?

YOUR UNIQUE JOURNEY

If my lesson about these important relationships isn't high priority for you at this moment, you might use pages 201–8 to brainstorm and recall other instructive stories and experiences from your unique life journey.

13

No Fences

KNOCKING DOWN BARRIERS

Injustice anywhere is a threat to justice everywhere.

Dr. Martin Luther King, Jr.

Though my family never stayed in the same place for long, my grandfather's home in Ozark, Missouri, was the place I really considered home. I always knew that, if one day everything fell apart, I could return to my grandpa's house. My family dates to the founding of Ozark, and seven generations of my family have lived in this home. My great-grandfathers built the mill around which the town grew. They'd been prosperous merchants but lost everything—except the house—in the Great Depression.

When I was growing up, my grandpa's house had ornate wrought iron bars on the windows. To me they seemed a natural and necessary part of the structure, even though no other house in town had them. The neighborhood was safe, so the bars served no discernable function. I was shocked the day I learned their purpose.

One spring I was moving rocks out of Grandpa's half-acre garden when I discovered a strange-looking stone. It was flat and damaged, about a foot long and eight or ten inches wide. It looked artificial among the natural stones I was lifting out of the soil.

This stone had a woman's name on it.

Horrified, it dawned on me that I may have discovered a grave in the garden. I ran frantically to my grandfather. When he saw why I was so upset, he couldn't contain his laughter. He collected himself and shared a story from the Great Depression, when many people couldn't afford funeral services or nice grave sites. The county created a paupers' cemetery for them. Their headstones were scraps of tin with the deceased's name nail-punched into it. This "engraved" tin was then secured to a piece of wood to serve as a grave marker.

Most cemeteries at that time had fences to separate the paid side from the paupers' side. Since the paupers' grave markers weren't intended to last, the fence separated the haves from the have-nots and ensured that no "worthy" citizen was unintentionally buried on top of the destitute. Sounds a lot like lunch tickets for eternity.

Great-Grandfather Earnest knew that, once the tin markers disappeared, the unmarked side of the graveyard would become just another paupers' field, like many such unmarked cemeteries throughout rural America. Earnest took it upon himself to create headstones by pouring concrete blocks and placing hand-carved wooden letters into the wet concrete, spelling each person's name and date. One by one he replaced the tin markers with these sturdy concrete markers. The one I'd found had accidentally broken when removed from the frame and had been discarded.

I sat dumbfounded, amazed by my great-grandfather's resolve and achievement. Nobody paid him. No committee charged him with the task. He just decided to act.

Then my grandfather said, "More important than that—you see those metal bars on our windows? Those used to be part of the fence that separated the paid cemetery from the paupers' cemetery."

That ornate fence separating the two cemeteries had made Earnest angry. His own financial collapse created in him a passion to ensure that people were respected, regardless of social or economic class. That would mark the remainder of his life. He recognized this fence as a symbol of the way people were separated by money, even in death. After installing all the headstones, Earnest removed the barrier by hand. To show how strongly he despised how the fence dehumanized the poor, Great-Grandfather Earnest not only removed it—he cut it into segments and mounted them on his windows. This was his public statement against segregation and disrespect.

After reading my great-grandfather's writings and talking to some of his contemporaries, I now know he was never worried that, when his time came, he was going to end up on the paupers' side; our family had acquired plots for future generations on the paid side. All Earnest wanted was to help build a better world for his children and grandchildren. He knew we could do that only by creating that world in our day.

Our family home is still occupied by a family member. It has been remodeled many times, and the bars have been removed. But a three-foot panel of those bars, with its faded gold fleur-de-lis and rust overtaking the original black paint, has a place of honor in my home office as a reminder of my responsibility to continue fighting the disrespect Earnest so publicly disavowed. It's my responsibility to lift people up and tear down barriers that keep people separated and excluded.

My great-grandfather's story reminds me that great leaders don't just repaint fences to improve the view; they tear them down. They don't merely assume a wall exists for a good reason; they challenge and change the conditions that made the barrier seem necessary in the first place.

ALWAYS FORWARD

- What fences need to be torn down to make your community better? What are you waiting for?
- Whom can you invite to bring resources and help with your mission?

YOUR UNIQUE JOURNEY

You are welcome to apply my fences lesson in your life, or maybe your story wants to teach you something more important for this moment. On pages 201–8 I've provided a list of categories and prompts that might help you brainstorm and remember instructive stories and experiences.

14

CEO of Your Own Responsibilities

LEADING LIKE AN OWNER

> Do not just delegate tasks to the next genera-
> tion. If you delegate tasks, you create followers.
> Instead, delegate authority to create leaders.
>
> Craig Groeschel

Throughout most of my career I have been the point leader. Whether I held the title CEO, president, executive direc-
tor, or business owner, I've found myself in a position of leadership. That station comes with lofty expectations from the world around me. My behaviors and results affect not only me but every person on my team, my board of directors, and others in my sphere of influence. However, as most of you know, fulfilling great expectations leads to great reward. And I want others to experience the benefits I enjoy as CEO.

Freedom sounds scary to a lot of leaders. This is illustrated in one of my favorite Bible stories, the parable of the talents (Matt. 25:14–30), in which the master embarks on a long journey and entrusts three servants with managing portions of his wealth while he is gone. I've always believed that parable is about two leadership factors: empowerment and capacity. The master expects high outcomes from each of the three, but he also understands the abilities of each. He trusts each servant with a different amount—a little, a middle, and a lot—expecting each to maximize his resources.

I find myself often using this story's principles to coach team members, outside clients, and my daughter. Guiding them to maximize their careers and impact requires that I look carefully at each person's capacity. We all bring different talents and strengths to an organization. As a leader I strive to give every team member access to all the resources he or she needs. But that's not enough. Team members need empowerment to *use* available resources. When people join our team, they're all given keys to every office, credit cards, access to all the organization's files (except confidential personnel files), and responsibility to use them wisely. Ample resources are wonderful, but team members can only achieve excellence when we empower them to make CEO-level decisions and take action using those resources.

Since Southwest Michigan First makes each team member a CEO of his or her own responsibilities, salaried team members don't use forms for requesting and approving time away. We don't track when people leave for a few hours here and there for children's appointments or a spouse's work event. As the company's CEO I don't have to account for my time use at that level; similarly my people are CEOs of their own responsibilities, and we give them the same freedom. This fosters high responsibility and leads to strong results. Scottish advertising genius David Ogilvy said, "If each of us hires people who are bigger than we are, we shall become a company of giants."[1]

However, we do account for performance and outcomes. Every team member understands that, along with a CEO's freedoms, they bear the weight of a CEO's responsibilities. When your people act as CEOs of their responsibilities, they help take your organization to the next level, and you'll find yourself with a team of highly engaged individuals.

Steve Jobs said, "A small team of A+ players can run circles around a giant team of B and C players."[2] I love this quote. As a leader I have tons of reasons for wanting to be around A players. Here are a few.

One, A players push others to be better. They're constantly striving for greatness but not necessarily competing. A players build innovatively on what others are doing, always raising the bar. Curl up with Ed Catmull's book *Creativity, Inc.* It's all about putting amazing, creative people in a room and letting them do remarkable things together. They are constantly challenging each other to produce something far superior to the sum of its individual parts.

Two, from a simple management standpoint, A players create fewer problems. We don't have a human resources director at Southwest Michigan First because we have amazing people. We don't spend a lot of time tracking people's work hours or days off. Instead we hire high-performance people who produce much more than those who just punch a clock.

We've had past problems when we've hired people because we liked them or because they needed jobs but they didn't necessarily perform at an A level. This is one reason we've developed such a meticulous, well-organized hiring strategy. Otherwise I would end up hiring everyone who applied. I love everybody I meet for one reason or another, and I want to give everyone a shot at being awesome. What I've learned, though, is that I often want more for people than they want for themselves. Regardless of personal feelings, we must be strategic and hire only A players.

Throughout my career I've seen great people leave great organizations for one of only two reasons. Either the new opportunity advanced their leadership impact or they didn't want to work with a B player closely aligned with them. You see, even one B player brings down the average of the whole team, and great people don't want to be part of that. A players want to work with equally amazing, driven, exciting people.

● ● ●

A few years ago I had the distinct privilege of spending the day with Horst Schulze, former president and chief operating officer of Ritz-Carlton. It was one of the most impactful days of my leadership career. It furthered my journey and reinforced my belief that great organizations are fundamentally a function of trust and engagement. Horst shared that Ritz-Carlton is deliberate about the strengths and talents of those they hire. The reason the company is considered best in customer service is not that it pays people more—in fact, it pays about the same as its competitors—but that it's the best in training and trust.

Every Ritz-Carlton employee understands that they are "Ladies and Gentlemen serving Ladies and Gentlemen."[3] All thirty-five thousand employees have the authority to spend up to two thousand dollars to solve a customer's problem and ensure that a Ritz-Carlton customer is a customer for life. I asked Horst how they could take such a risk with every employee. His response was classic Horst Schulze: "How could we not do it? Our average customer spends $250,000 with us in their lifetime."

In addition to knowing they're empowered and part of an incredible team, employees discuss in each day's shift meeting one of Ritz-Carlton's twelve service values, which every employee carries on a pocket card:

1. I build strong relationships and create Ritz-Carlton guests for life.
2. I am always responsive to the expressed and unexpressed wishes and needs of our guests.
3. I am empowered to create unique, memorable, and personal experiences for our guests.
4. I understand my role in achieving the Key Success Factors, embracing Community Footprints, and creating The Ritz-Carlton Mystique.
5. I continuously seek opportunities to innovate and improve The Ritz-Carlton experience.
6. I own and immediately resolve guest problems.
7. I create a work environment of teamwork and lateral service so that the needs of our guests and each other are met.
8. I have the opportunity to continuously learn and grow.
9. I am involved in the planning of the work that affects me.

10. I am proud of my professional appearance, language, and behavior.

11. I protect the privacy and security of our guests, my fellow employees, and the company's confidential information and assets.

12. I am responsible for uncompromising levels of cleanliness and creating a safe and accident-free environment.[4]

The Ritz-Carlton may not call its team members "CEOs of their own responsibilities," but its people sure act that way. With its commitment to empowering and trusting its team, it's no wonder Ritz-Carlton has become the standard to which companies around the globe aspire.

● ● ●

But there are times this doesn't work. My leadership has been radically shaped by having to fire teammates. I've employed hundreds of people throughout my career, but I'll never forget the first time I had to let someone go. It started when we promised to provide a client with a few hundred custom-produced, autographed books for gifts at a convention. The individually inscribed copies were to be placed in each guest's hotel room on the first day of the conference. On the last day the CEO of the client company called to explain in no uncertain terms how disappointed he was in me and my organization. We had not fulfilled our commitment; his guests never received the books, upon which he had based his entire closing remarks at the conference.

I don't remember my exact words, but I promised to make it right no matter what it required.

Why had we failed to come through? The reason still haunts me. Joyce, who was leading this project, got busy on the first day of the conference and "just ran out of time" to make the delivery. Why hadn't she delivered the books on day two or three? She replied, "I thought the problem would just go away."

Over the next two days we called every conference attendee, apologized for our mistake, and arranged to deliver the books overnight. Our client appreciated our efforts and the money we lost in shipping, but they never hired us again.

The real pain was yet to come. As the saying goes, "It's not the crime but the cover-up that gets you in trouble." I had to talk to Joyce. That morning, when I arrived at work, the dread caused me to empty my stomach's contents into the trash can. I knew firing Joyce meant more than just the loss of her job; it would impact her family, her relationships, and her future employability. She was a friend, but I couldn't let her continue on the team. She had damaged our reputation and put at risk the prospects of the whole team and their families. When she missed the deadline, we could have addressed and fixed the problem. But she didn't humble herself and own it. She didn't ask for help. That effort would have cost the team some time, but nowhere near the ultimate cost we incurred. We never got the chance to fix the problem together, because Joyce didn't take responsibility for her important role.

The pain of telling a trusted teammate she could no longer work with us, that she had lost the team's and our client's confidence, and that I could no longer trust her—it was overwhelming. I was completely wrecked afterward. Firing is, for me, the hardest part of leadership, but leaders must all eventually let people go.

Blake Mycoskie, founder of Toms Shoes, says, "You've got to prune your organization of people who violate company trust. This can be difficult, but it must be done. This goes especially for high-performing employees. In the long run, the success of your company is not based on the two highest-performing employees, but on the trust you create within your entire organization. Company culture must be maintained at all costs."[5]

Mistakes happen. A few years ago someone dropped the ball for our annual leadership conference, Catalyst University. But instead of covering up or ignoring the problem, our team immediately addressed it. Our guests were never the wiser. This confirmed that expecting people to be CEOs of their own responsibilities is the only way I ever want to lead.

ALWAYS FORWARD

- How can you and your team take responsibility for your failures in order to ensure success in the future?
- What are you empowering your team members to achieve?
- What freedoms will support their sense of personal responsibility?

YOUR UNIQUE JOURNEY

If you need to focus on becoming or helping each of your people become a CEO of one's own responsibilities, go for it. If, on the other hand, your life is teaching you something even more important, consider using pages 201–8 to guide your exploration of your unique experience.

15

Family First

KNOW WHAT MATTERS

> Your leadership of your family will grow in direct
> proportion to the love that you show your family.
>
> Mark Merrill

Years ago my family vacationed on South Padre Island with my wife's extended family. We'd been looking forward to this trip for months. We rented a beach house, and it should have been a special time. But after two days I started getting frantic calls from the office. A huge deal that my team had been trying to close was rapidly falling apart. In a panic I left my family mid-vacation and flew home in a desperate attempt to piece things back together. I missed a week of precious moments and memories to secure a deal that, despite my efforts, died anyway. Truth is, I knew it was never meant to happen.

My wife, Lyn, has a photo from that trip in which I'm talking on my cell phone, pacing on the beach. Any photos from that trip trigger embarrassment. I wish I'd never left my family for something so trivial. But it taught me a significant lesson and caused me to reorganize my priorities around the idea of "family first."

At the time I didn't think I had permission to say no. When we began to build Southwest Michigan First, I saw this sentiment in my team as well. No one questioned me, the "boss," when I left at 3:30 p.m. for a child's school event. But I started noticing others didn't feel comfortable doing the same, or were apologetic about asking for family time. Frankly, I felt like a dictator, knowing people came to me, guilt-ridden, for permission to fulfill their responsibilities as parents or spouses. I decided each team member should be empowered to make those scheduling decisions for themselves; nobody else in the world bears a person's responsibility of caring for his or her family.

We give people leave to tell their team, "Hey, I'm going to be out at three for my kid's track meet! If you need me, call." That lifts up the individual and also lifts all of us, because we get to celebrate and share in that family's success. Our closeness creates a family environment.

In today's world we're constantly connected through laptops, smartphones, and tablets. That can mean we're constantly working. We expect team members to attend work-related events or client meetings during nights and weekends, so we choose to put families first. Our interconnections in our teams allow many responsibilities to be shared. If you need someone to cover your phone while you're out, we can do that. But no one else can go to your child's spelling bee

119

for you. No one else can replace you in that classroom where you help struggling readers each week.

To ensure our team understands commitment to family, we developed a strategy borrowed from Andy Stanley, the great leadership and faith leader. In his book *Choosing to Cheat*, he insists that no one has permission to cheat their family. At Southwest Michigan First, *Choosing to Cheat* is the foundation of our family-first policy. Schedule conflicts mean somebody is going to be cheated, forcing a choice about who that will be. I like to make that choice easy. If someone has to be cheated, let that somebody be me. We will rebound, I promise. I'm not talking about moral cheating. I expect you to choose your family's genuine needs over work. I expect you to stay home to care for your sick child. If you come to work, your mind won't really be there anyway.

I regularly get emails that ask, "What do you do if somebody abuses this policy?" It never happens. When you hire amazing people, they don't abuse their team members. A fully engaged team, committed to individual and organizational success, won't misuse the system.

Engaged teams openly share their calendars, including mine. I don't mark family events private; anyone can see them.

PepsiCo Australia and New Zealand calls their strategy "leaders leaving loudly." To put families first, all team members are expected to announce they are leaving and where they're going. CEO Robert Rietbroek, who developed the strategy, shared, "I'd like you to be a hero at work, but I want you to be a hero at home. If you're only a hero at work, you're only doing half the job."[1]

Patagonia, the clothing and equipment company, is famous for automatically locking the doors to their Ventura,

California, headquarters at 8:00 p.m. And they don't reopen until morning, when their daycare opens.

● ● ●

The most common pushback I receive about family first is that not all jobs have the flexibility to allow such self-management. True. If you're an emergency room nurse, people die if you're not at your post. Also, nearly everyone has times when they can't break away. Family first is about planning and committing as much as possible to the reality that, if you left your job tomorrow, in a day or week or month the organization would replace you. But no one can replace you as a parent or spouse.

Family first is also about personally embracing our teammates and families. Southwest Michigan First is currently in a season of babies. I love babies visiting work. They add energy and excitement to the office and draw our team closer. Then we're all more willing to pull together when a team member needs support.

Rich Sheridan, the founder of Menlo Innovations, has taken the idea of family to a new level by allowing his team members to bring their babies to work, not once a year, but every day. Recently, with four children in the office, the only distraction was team members wanting to hold the babies—not change them, just hold them. I assure you, Rich doesn't worry about losing talented parents to his competitors.

According to Gallup, at a typical organization in America only 30 percent of employees are "actively engaged," meaning they see the organization's success as their success and will do everything they can to exceed expectations. In contrast, nearly half of all employees fall into the "disengaged" category—that is, their work is just a job they shut off when they walk out the door at five o'clock. They put in the hours but not much more. The most dangerous group in the typical organization is the remaining 20 percent, who are "actively disengaged." These people are miserable in their jobs and take joy in sharing their misery with anyone.

As employees or consumers, we have all experienced actively disengaged organizations. The service is awful, the product quality is bad, and we leave with relief. In college I received the gift of working for such an organization. I say "gift" because the experience showed me the dark side—to which I never want to return. Half the employees stole from the company and the other half looked the other way. The manager freely shared his management philosophy: "maximum anxiety." He wanted employees alternating between fear and hatred toward him. His favorite quote was from Casey Stengel: "The key to being a good manager is keeping the people who hate me away from those who are still undecided."[2]

You can imagine the customer experience and the constant employee turnover. Those hardwired to be actively engaged won't stay in an actively disengaged workplace. The day I left this company was one of the best in my career. I vowed to do all in my power to never again work in such an environment.

Southwest Michigan First's team engagement scores hover between 95 and 100 percent, for which we've been recognized by the *Wall Street Journal*,[3] *Outside* magazine,[4] and Best and Brightest[5] as one of the best places to work in America. This has created not only a happier workplace but also tremendous customer satisfaction and higher margins.

We've studied great organizations, and when asked what makes an organization great, team members don't point to salary or financial perks, as we might expect. Most important are the love, support, and nurturing they and their families receive. They're embraced for who and where they are and allowed to own their life balance.

Today great organizations must also ensure that team members without spouses or children feel the same support for their needs. They can't validate their absences by sick children or sporting events. But most of them have other passions, and we can engage with those. Whether an employee is tutoring a child, pursuing education, supporting elderly parents, or partaking in charitable activities that feed their souls, engagement is about giving people capacity to manage their own lives. This further empowers them to act as CEOs of their own responsibilities and rise to high expectations.

I, the point leader, must show that I actively participate in a balanced life. If team members observe me engaging with my family or going to the gym at midday, it reinforces "family first" as part of our culture, not just a bullet point in our recruitment package. If the point leader doesn't lead by example, no one else in the organization will believe they have permission to live a healthy balance of responsibilities.

ALWAYS FORWARD

- Where have you seen people pick work or other responsibility over family, only to discover later that their efforts made little or no impact on the organization's success?

- What three things would you add or change in your organization to make it more family friendly? What is holding you back?
- If you were CEO, what would you change in your work-life integration? How can you make that happen, regardless of your title?

YOUR UNIQUE JOURNEY

If it fits, please run with my family-first lesson in your life and leadership. But if your life is trying to teach you a different lesson, you may wish to use pages 201–8 to help you brainstorm and remember instructive stories and experiences.

16

Be Original

DON'T FAKE YOUR LIFE

Celebrate your existence!
William Blake

N ever sit at the head of the table. Someone more important might show up, and you'll be embarrassed when
they ask you to move." This paraphrase of Jesus's teaching
on humility (see Luke 14:7–11) is true and wise, but many
leaders misapply it and fail to take leadership opportunities
that require visibility and prominence. An effective leader
can stand boldly in the spotlight without sacrificing humility. Humility is in one's attitude about self and others, and
doesn't necessarily require invisibility.

Many of us have heard that great leaders don't draw attention to themselves or that servant leadership means staying
in the back of the room and never in the spotlight. In his
book *Good to Great*, Jim Collins discusses level-five leaders

and their traits of shyness and humility. While these concepts have merit, they are too often misunderstood and used as an excuse for inaction and absentee leadership.

Today's economy requires leaders who understand that their personal brand is a direct reflection on their organization and influences people's willingness to engage with the leader and their product, service, church, or organization. Before choosing to join your tribe, your customers want to know your organization's leaders and their values. They want to see leaders revealing themselves authentically. Whether you're a consumer brand, church, government, or educational leader, people want to know who they will have to trust and, when there is a problem, who will advocate for them.

We live in a star-focused system that doesn't reward invisible leaders. We can no longer hide our leadership light in the back of the room.

"Regardless of age, regardless of position, regardless of the business we happen to be in, all of us need to understand the importance of branding. We are CEOs of our own companies: Me Inc. To be in business today, our most important job is to be head marketer for the brand called You."[1] These words from Tom Peters truly changed my perspective and the direction of my leadership.

Today, more than ever, each of us has more opportunity to build our own brand, and it has never been more critical that we do so. The good news is that building a personal brand is not reserved for an organization point leader. Everyone has the ability and responsibility to grow their brand.

You are not defined by your job title or job description. It's up to you how and when you present yourself. But how do you begin?

Authenticity Rules

Authentic is the opposite of fake. I remember driving across the country, from Missouri to California, with my mother and brother and stopping for gas at a combination restaurant, gas station, and Native American gift store (or, as my brother and I called it, a "rubber snake store"). My grandfather had given me a little money for the trip, and I set my heart on a "genuine, authentic" tomahawk. I was six or seven, so the rubber head on my new genuine, authentic tomahawk seemed more a safety feature, not a reason to question its provenance. What crushed my spirit and forever ruined my quest for a rubber snake store tomahawk was the tiny sticker that read, "Made in Taiwan." It's the little things that kill authenticity.

I am fascinated by people who challenge the status quo, who don't let other people's preconceptions determine their future. Misty Copeland, arguably America's greatest ballerina, grew up in a dysfunctional family and didn't start ballet until her teens. She admits she doesn't look like other dancers. But she has used her differentness to propel herself and her dance company to heights perhaps never before achieved in American dance. Though she excelled in her early career, some companies dismissed her because she didn't look like their ideal dancer. But the American Ballet Theatre saw greatness, and in 2015 she became the first African American woman promoted to principal dancer in the organization's seventy-five-year history.

Why has Misty Copeland become one of the world's most famous dancers? Because people value originals and, conversely, flee from fakes.

Early in my career I struggled with coveting the ultimate sign of success: a fancy watch. I was wearing a watch that I bought at a convenience store counter; a Rolex was not in my immediate future. Then a business trip to Asia introduced me to knockoff watches, and I jumped at the chance of owning my own "Rolex." A few days after returning, as I was proudly sporting my new bling, a member of my board asked to talk privately. He bluntly said, "You are not helping yourself with the fake watch. Given your age, people won't believe it's real. And if you're lying about your watch, why should we trust you with important things?" He went on to explain the cost of knockoff goods to our economy and that, by participating, I was stealing from the designers and their employees.

I threw that watch in the trash before we left the meeting, feeling embarrassed with a little self-loathing thrown in. A day later that same board member showed up and gave me a modest watch, on the back of which he'd inscribed, "I am proud of you."

The world will reward you for being an original. You'll never receive much respect for being a knockoff. People fill arenas to see Bono and U2, not the bar bands that play their songs. Berkshire Hathaway chairman Warren Buffet recently held an auction for his annual charity lunch, where a fan paid $3 million to dine with the nerdy CEO from Nebraska. Why? For the same reason 44,000 people show up at his annual shareholders' meeting and tens of thousands listen online. For an amazing read on originality, see his annual letter to shareholders.

With the world's information in our hands via smartphones, it's not knowledge alone we crave. We want authentic *application* of that knowledge. This largely explains the exponential growth of social mission companies such as Toms Shoes or Warby Parker Glasses. I've recently purchased several buy-one-give-one products—not to support the related charities but because I've gotten to know the companies' leaders and appreciate their authentic commitment to their products, customers, and beneficiaries.

In a world where Glassdoor reports on workplace authenticity, Rate My Professor evaluates teachers, and Yelp reviews churches, you can't fake authenticity.

Be Known for Something That Inspires Others

Bob Goff is one of my heroes—not because he's sold over a million books, or because he's flown food transports into some of the world's most dangerous places, or even because he has helped thousands learn to read through schools he's funded. Bob is my hero because he loves better than anyone I've met. Of course, Bob loves easy-to-love people: his family and friends, church leaders, and fans who fill conference centers and churches to hear him. But what makes Bob special is his love for people we—or at least I—would define as unlovable. Like the street gang members who broke into his car and stole the only manuscript of his second book. He loves the witch doctors with whom he works in Uganda, who are pure evil until they experience Bob's love. Bob inspires me to love better.

There are inspirational people all around you, and you trust them and want to interact with them and their organizations. I am blessed in this area; one of our companies organizes conferences and meetings all over the country. I get to select the speakers and presenters, which means I get to know the people who inspire me by the ways they live, overcome obstacles, and serve in leadership.

In truth, when I meet these women and men, I'm usually a little intimidated because I know them from their "highlight reel." After getting to know them in person, I still find myself in awe of their character and can't hold back my enthusiasm to help them inspire others. I'm thinking of people like Inky Johnson, whose bad break on the football field left him physically damaged but who chose a positive attitude that soars. Or Hannah Brencher, who turned her loneliness into a cause that sends tens of thousands of love letters to people around the globe—people who need to know that others care and that they're not forgotten.

You don't need to scale Everest or produce a number-one album to inspire people. You just need to do something—anything—that inspires others to be more, do more, and love more than they did before.

Look in the Mirror

"There are only two things that can derail your leadership: a fiduciary failure or a moral failure. You must be on constant guard against both of these." A board member gave me this advice over a private dinner celebrating my ten years leading our businesses. This man was (and is) a globally renowned business leader and philanthropist, and my greatest mentor. He shared this warning not because of anything I had done but because of behaviors and consequences he'd observed in his career as a CEO, chairperson, and board member in dozens of companies.

Each of us can probably name dozens of leaders whose lives and organizations have been destroyed not because of limited abilities but because of their choices. Enlightened leaders understand their vulnerabilities and create systems to avoid or minimize temptation. They ensure their behavior is above reproach, because they understand the cost of failure.

Be Teacher, Guide, and Advocate

Whenever he quoted Zig Ziglar, my grandfather would start, "As ole Zig would say. . . " Years later I figured out that Zig was a generation younger than Gramps. I learned a lot of lessons from Zig on the front porch swing, but the one I've never forgotten is his refrain, "You can have everything in life you want if you will just help enough other people get what they want."[2] This saying became ole Zig's brand; he was the man who wanted you to thrive so he could as well.

I believe that, if he were still with us, Zig Ziglar would change his mantra to include: "You can have anything you want in this world if you just mentor enough people on *how to use what they have* to succeed." Zig's world was a time of scarcity, as opposed to today, when we have such an abundance of information, access, and resources. What people crave—and what preeminent brands have—is knowledge of *what to do* with those resources.

As a leader, you are a manager of knowledge, and you can build your knowledge management brand in many ways. You can become overwhelmed with the abundance of information and have trouble deciding where to focus. The key is to capitalize on areas where you have real-world knowledge.

To have impact and build your brand, you must know where your audience hangs out. Are they YouTube people or podcast people? Do they read blogs or tweets? There are dozens of conduits through which you can teach. The key is to be consistent, credible (stay focused in your area), and knowledgeable. Bring insights in a simple format that people can digest and utilize in their leadership.

"Brand" is not a logo; it's a collection of perceptions about you in the minds of people who care. It's this simple: you are a brand. And you are in charge of your brand. There is no single path to success.

You can't treat your brand as an afterthought. It's your core differentiator. Personal brands differentiate between individuals, allowing some to increase their value and the value that their patrons perceive in their organizations. Your customers will enjoy great experiences only if you understand your unique value and deliver on it every day with the highest possible quality.

ALWAYS FORWARD

- Want to know what your current brand is?
  - Write your obituary.
  - Ask your spouse, your boss, and a friend to write your obituary.
- In fifteen words or less, write a summary of your brand. Do not include your titles or roles, just what is remarkable and distinctive.

- What do you want to be famous for? For Bob Goff, it's love.
- Where in your life can you step out of the shadows and allow your light to shine?

YOUR UNIQUE JOURNEY

You are welcome to apply my lesson on originality in your life, or maybe your story wants to teach you something more important for this moment. On pages 201–8 I've provided a list of categories and prompts that might help you brainstorm and remember instructive stories and experiences.

17

Action over Emotion

KICK FEAR IN THE FACE

Fear will shout about who you were; love will
whisper about who we are becoming. Listen to
the truest voice, not the loudest one.

Bob Goff

Once I had the wonderful opportunity to go on a retreat
called The Walk to Emmaus. Participants had to look
deep within themselves and address whatever was holding
them back from being their greatest selves, the persons God
put on this earth to succeed.

I'd never really thought about this before. But when I
looked, I found that fear was holding me back—fear that
people would find out how poor I'd grown up, that I had
climbed inside Goodwill boxes for clothes. I was afraid people

134

could take away what I'd achieved—my sense of well-being—merely on a whim.

That fear had become debilitating to me. I discovered I had been more concerned about keeping my secret than about achieving the purpose God has set in my heart. This realization set me on a new journey, and I resolved never again to hold back. I had to be open to sharing the stories of my childhood. I could no longer pretend I'd gone to the right schools and had a typical four-year college experience. I had to be vulnerable and expose my authentic self. I was terrified.

Translating such a realization into a dramatic life change doesn't happen overnight. When you're a family's breadwinner, you worry about keeping your job, not just to prevent derailing your career but to keep your family safe. You need health care for your children and food on the table.

I know firsthand what it's like to live without these basics. When I grew up, I felt the sting of lacking health care, or even food at times. I remember once, when I'd hurt my knee, checking into a hospital under my cousin's address, because he lived in a county with better public health care. I also remember eating government cheese and peanut butter provided through welfare programs. I never wanted to repeat those experiences (even though the cheese was really good).

But I started naming my fears and revealing them to people: "Here's what I'm most afraid of. Here are the things that keep me awake at night." And the fear would evaporate like fog in the midday sun.

I shared my fears with my management coach, and he asked, "Well, what would you do if you were fired tomorrow?"

I had recently spent a personal day at Martha's Vineyard. I'd seen thousands of Black Dog T-shirts over the years, sporting a black Labrador retriever, and I wanted to visit the hamburger joint they advertised: the Black Dog Tavern. Mostly, I wanted to understand why so many people wore the shirts. When I arrived, I discovered the gift shop was several times larger than the restaurant. The "tavern" was really a T-shirt business that happened to sell beer and burgers! I became fascinated by their business model.

So I answered my coach, "You know what? I'd start a business like the Black Dog Tavern!" My dog, Truman, the world's greatest Labrador retriever, happens to be a white lab. So I said, "I would sell tacos and beer, and I would sell lots of T-shirts with Truman's picture on them."

I was half-joking, but my coach said, "You should write a business plan for that."

I had written and reviewed hundreds of business plans, so I wrote one for Truman's Tacos and Beer. We discussed the plan, and my coach asked, "Could you live on what that business would make?"

"Yeah. I could do that."

"Well, then, you don't have to be fearful anymore. Now you know that, if you lost your job tomorrow, you could still take care of your family. At present your job is to put enough money in savings so you can start that company any time you want."

That eased my fear, which finally dissolved entirely the day I'd put away enough savings that I could launch the venture. My ego was no longer at risk. Adequate food or health care was no longer at risk. Though I never actually started this business, I annually throw a Truman's Tacos and Beer party to celebrate my victory over fear. I invite my team, board members, clients, and supporters, and I share my story. If I could deal with that fear, other leaders surely can also face it down. Every year we design a new T-shirt. And we've diversified from just tacos—I've done a Low Country shrimp boil the last two years. But no matter the menu, I love to bring people together around this idea—that anyone can choose to be either a victim of change or an agent of change. Though you sometimes can't control circumstances, your response is all in your hands. But first you must make the decision to own your future and not allow fear to paralyze you.

● ● ●

I've always believed that a job is the greatest force for change, so employment was fundamental to my confidence. That's the main reason I feared unemployment. My job had become my identity, and losing my job meant losing myself. I was not born to live in this fear.

Fear is as old as time, it seems. The command not to be afraid appears in the Bible more than eighty times. I'm reminded of the Dale Carnegie quote: "Inaction breeds doubt and fear. Action breeds confidence and courage. If you want to conquer fear, do not sit home and think about it. Go out and get busy."[1] You can't maneuver around your leadership fears; you have to go through them.

Leaders of all ages, genders, and backgrounds regularly write or call about what is holding them back. Their patterns generally fall into a few categories.

One, imposter syndrome. This involves fear that people will discover you're not Superman, and they'll no longer value you. I certainly fit this category. Paulo Coelho writes in the voice of the alchemist, "There is just one thing that makes your dream become impossible: the fear of failure."[2]

Two, fear of not being prepared. I regularly see young leaders who procrastinate because they don't feel ready. News flash: no one feels ready before they start. As Amy March says in Louisa May Alcott's novel *Little Women*, "I'm not afraid of storms, for I'm learning how to sail my ship."[3]

Three, fear of the unknown. This is the fear that keeps good from becoming great. It traps people in bad relationships, jobs, and neighborhoods. I recently visited the oldest bullfighting ring in Spain. The tour guide shared that in a bullfight every bull has its own *carencia*, the spot to which it returns when it feels threatened. The bull repeatedly comes back to this spot, believing familiarity means safety. But in the Spanish arena, as in our lives, safety is truly found in change.

Four, lack of planning. General George Patton dealt with fear through believing that "The time to take counsel of your fears is before you make an important battle decision. That's the time to listen to every fear you can imagine! When you have collected all of the facts and fears and made your decision, turn off all your fears and go ahead!"[4] Sounds like the general would enjoy consuming Truman's Tacos and Beer with me.

Five, fear overcoming mission. Too many times, we as leaders have a burning passion, a true mission to be a force for change. But we allow our fears, that little voice in our head, to speak louder than the mission in our heart. I love the Millennial generation for their passion around purpose and mission. This kind of focus enables us to overcome fear.

Nothing great ever happened to someone who knew every step, action, and outcome at their journey's start. W. Clement Stone said, "When thinking won't cure fear, action will."[5]

ALWAYS FORWARD

- What fears are holding you back?
- Can you identify the source of these? How can you address them?
- If you were to proceed in spite of fear, what three things would you attempt?

YOUR UNIQUE JOURNEY

You might need to deal with fear in your life and leadership. If so, this chapter's lesson is for you. But if not, ask what other lesson your unique life experience is trying to teach you. Maybe pages 201–8 will help.

18

Protecting Joy

EDIT YOUR LIFE FOR EXCELLENCE

Self-care is not selfish. Self-care is strategic.

Mike Foster

No matter how well your life journey is going, there will be dirty, rotten, horrible, terrible, bad days. The key to sustaining your leadership is to keep these days from becoming a pattern and stealing your joy. I hit this point eight years ago. Someone noticed and asked, "What happened to your joy? I know you love this place as much as I do, but you would never know it by your actions." This punch in the face did not come from a member of my board, a close friend, or a family member, but from a twenty-four-year-old team member with the courage to hold me accountable for my attitude and treatment of others.

That following Saturday morning came an unexpected knock at our door. It was my neighbor, a respected surgeon.

Lyn and I had dined with him and his wife the previous evening. He asked to talk privately. Once seated in my home office, with zero preamble he said he was worried about me. "You've lost your joy. How can I help?" I felt my friend's love during the two hours we trekked through my current life load. We eventually agreed that I had to come up with a plan.

I spent that Sunday trying to figure out what it was with these people, trying to convince me that something was amiss in my life. Why were they trying to hold me back? Didn't they understand that I was trying to change the world?

Monday, for the first time ever, I didn't want to go to work. I felt overwhelming dread. I kept thinking of the study that said that more people die on Mondays due to the emotional weight of starting a new work week. How had I gotten here?

I called the office and canceled my day. I wasn't sure when I would be in.

I started driving with no destination. A hundred miles later, somewhere in Indiana, I found myself parked on the shoulder, crying for no apparent reason. My tears subsided, and I looked up. A few hundred feet down the road stood an insurance billboard that had seen better days. Two-thirds of it was missing. The only words I could make out were "Call Your Friend." But I couldn't think of a single person I could call and tell honestly how lost I felt.

I believe some people receive unmistakably clear messages from God, but I never have. For me, His guidance feels more like holy prompts, and on that day He prompted me through a nearly collapsed billboard. The experience would prove life-altering.

Cars sped by, two stopping to see if I was alright. I spent the next hour talking to God about where I was and who

141

I wanted to be. Hunger came calling, and at a local diner outside West Lafayette, Indiana, I ate a pork tenderloin sandwich bigger than its platter. In the adjacent booth two men in construction clothes were talking about their lives. The older one shared a story I'd heard before, but today it was about me.

An old farmer receives a visit from a sheriff's deputy, who warns him of a coming storm that will cause the river to flood. He should evacuate.

The farmer replies, "The Lord will provide." He refuses to leave.

A few hours later the water has risen to the front porch. Someone comes with a boat to evacuate the farmer, but again he refuses. "The Lord will provide."

The water rises to the roof, and someone flies in with a helicopter to find the farmer sitting on his chimney. Again he declines the offer of help. "The Lord will provide."

The farmer drowns and goes to heaven. There he asks God, "What happened? I believed You would take care of me, that You would provide."

God replies, "I did provide. I sent a sheriff, a boat, and a helicopter."

I realized that God had sent me a twenty-four-year-old teammate, a surgeon, and a broken billboard. It was up to me to accept His help or face the death of my leadership and my joy.

Over my sandwich and a glass of iced tea I took inventory and mapped my new personal journey toward joy and alignment. In that café, on a dozen napkins, I listed everything I loved about my life, everything I valued—the people and things that were important to me, the ways I wanted to achieve impact. I painfully, honestly wrote my evaluation of my current progress in each area. I listed the actions to which I would commit to realign my life, so I would achieve the purpose for which I believe I was placed on this earth.

Over the next few weeks I met with people who were important to me and shared the journey on which I was embarking. I asked for their guidance, support, and accountability. I also told them about my friend who calls me each Yom Kippur to ask my forgiveness, in case he hurt me or our friendship over the past year. I wanted to do the same on my journey and asked their forgiveness. By the looks on some faces, I had a lot to repent for.

I should be clear. Business was great, and I had all the trappings of success. This was a crisis of abundance. Like a lot of entrepreneurial, growth-focused leaders, in my pursuit of the big things I'd forgotten to care for the small things. Like owning an expensive car but letting the oil run low and risking permanent engine damage.

My new journey began by reviewing my napkin notes, looking for common themes. As an annual physical reviews dozens of diagnostic data points to ensure whole-body health, I had to fine-tune my life by looking at all the minor changes required to achieve my ultimate goals. I hired a coach to help me work through the details of my leadership and life dreams and hold me accountable, to "raise the BS flag" when I failed to reach intermediate mileposts. Seven years later I still struggle with the issues that put me on the side of the road—self-respect, isolation, fear. But I've developed systems to address them and keep my life and leadership aligned.

I now know that I had all the symptoms of burnout, which, according to Dr. Sherrie Bourg Carter, are:

- Physical and emotional exhaustion
- Cynicism and detachment
- Feelings of ineffectiveness and lack of accomplishment[1]

Like a lot of type A personalities, I enjoy the drive and excitement of overcommitment. But on that roadside in Indiana I found that, like the finely crafted car that still dies without maintenance, I was suffering from lack of proper care and boundaries. I call these boundaries "riverbanks."

● ● ●

Whether you're an emerging or established leader, you must create riverbanks for your life. Flowing through my hometown is the Finley River, a beautiful, tree-lined waterway that once powered a grain mill. The mill pond served as the de facto community swimming pool. The river's banks were firm, supporting life both in the water and on land.

But that slowly changed. New homes upstream—with their lawns and chemicals in the runoff—changed the river's natural flow. When I was a kid, the river flooded its banks perhaps once in a lifetime. But now it floods every few years. It now resembles a swamp more than a river. Why? Because its banks became weak and gradually eroded. It no longer powers a mill or offers the pond's cooling waters for the summer heat.

That river has come to resemble my leadership. Even if a leader's mill is still grinding, he or she must be cautious of the incremental changes that can turn the river into a leadership swamp. This is why I've built and maintain riverbanks in my daily, weekly, monthly, and annual routines. These owe their existence to those café napkins.

Over the past decade I've interviewed more than one hundred leaders in business, philanthropy, faith, government, and education. I always ask about their routines and how they create riverbanks to protect them. I'm continually developing my leadership routines based on these mentorship moments.

As you learn about my riverbanks or those of other leaders you admire, know that you are unique and what serves one leader may or may not serve you in this season. Also note that you won't be able to implement every idea at once. That's a sure way to find yourself on the roadside, overwhelmed and looking for a pork cutlet. A few well-executed strategies are far more impactful than the mediocre execution of many.

My daily riverbanks start with my choice of bedtime. I haven't always believed in the healing power of sleep. I once told somebody, "I wish I could figure out a way to sleep less than six hours a day. Imagine what I could get done." Well, that's the equivalent of saying, "You know, if we polluted the river and killed off all the vegetation and fish, we could get more water to flow through." Rivers aren't meant to carry more water; they're meant to grow vegetation and fish. Sacrificing sleep for more achievement is self-defeating, but I thought that was how leadership worked. I believed that, if my Ambien lasted six hours, that was my body's way of telling me I needed only six hours of sleep. After all, I had a world to change.

Now I know my body requires a solid eight hours, and on weekends I'll probably get nine, maybe more, with a nap thrown in. I also know I'm nearly always going to wake up between six and six thirty in the morning. So bedtime is the critical decision. The Dalai Lama once said that "sleep is the best meditation."[2]

Awareness of your sleep needs is like knowing what type of fuel your car needs. My previous car could take E85 fuel, which contains a lot of alcohol and is less expensive. But my new car only runs on premium gas. It won't run on E85, no matter how much I'd like to save money. If I want to drive that car, I must use the correct fuel.

● ● ●

I'm not one of those people who can roll out of bed and fall to my knees in prayer. I was ten years old when the summer church camp minister told me, "If you don't pray first thing in the morning, you don't love Jesus." Ah, well . . . I'm going to give him a pass on his unbiblical advice. Maybe he was delirious after two weeks with ten-year-olds and no air-conditioning. I do believe that morning prayer is important, but my morning prayer is a celebration. I happen to love mornings. Yes, I'm that guy. Mornings are my time to thank the Lord for one more day to serve, to lead, and to learn. A sunrise to me is like the green light at a drag race—put the pedal down and go! But, to be clear, I believe it's okay with God that I have clean teeth, combed hair, and a cup of coffee before I meet with Him.

My prayers have always been more of a conversation than any kind of structured process. I make notes in advance as reminders to pray for friends, family, and situations. For some the note card thing seems a bit too structured, but it's important for me, as I don't want to tell someone, "I'll pray for you," then forget when pressures blur my memory.

My most common prayer location is our living room, sitting on the floor with Truman, the world's greatest Labrador retriever. We sit on the floor because Truman won't get on the furniture, and having him next to me gives me great comfort.

I start by praying for people. Tuesdays are special, as I specifically pray for each member of my team and their families—prayers of gratitude for their commitment to our work and for their allowing me to lead. I then usually spend five to ten minutes in thanksgiving and appreciation. After that I focus on meditation. I tend to center my meditation on one idea or thought, often from my Bible verse for the day. I use a meditation app—one of many available—that guides me through ten to fifteen minutes of pure focus and breathing. This preparation helps me find peace and make intentional decisions about where to focus my efforts for the day. And it prevents me from knee-jerk reacting or over-reacting to the unpredictable that will undoubtedly crop up later in the day.

The first time I sat down to quiet my mind, I made it about thirty seconds before the first thought intruded. So start small, with a few minutes, and build up to fifteen or twenty. I encourage you to give it a try. It will help you give yourself a little grace when you enter or reenter your day. You will enjoy more peace and increased capacity, better prepared for whatever the world ends up gifting you.

More often than not I reach a point where I empty my mind of thoughts, and I start to receive prompts that direct my day. At this point I've been sitting on the floor with

Truman for twenty to twenty-five minutes, and it's time to start moving and meet the day, rested, relaxed, and ready to change the world.

Prayer and meditation have become integral to my day, necessary for me to be the leader I expect to be, the leader those I serve need. If I, the point leader, am anxious and overwhelmed, I'm going to infect everyone with whom I interact. I will cast anxiety into their day even if everything I say is positive and correct. If I'm not calming and disciplined, I can kill productivity for the entire organization.

Peter Drucker said, "Follow effective action with quiet reflection. From the quiet reflection will come even more effective action."[3] Leaders need to lean into that truth. We all want to be effective. Setting aside twenty or thirty minutes can seem self-indulgent or wasteful, but, as I still must remind myself, self-care is no more wasteful than changing the oil in your car.

● ● ●

Another of my riverbanks is intentional time management. Every leader—in fact, probably every human on earth with any responsibilities—feels overwhelmed with time demands and the need to intentionally manage our choices for impact, rather than merely reacting to the loudest or squeakiest voice. Jim Collins writes, "Good is the enemy of great."[4] No matter how good your prioritizing is today, if you're not constantly changing and looking to be great at managing your time, you are falling behind. Most of us who believe we're good at managing time are in reality below average.

Like many of you, I struggle to resist the myth that the harder and more I work, the farther ahead I'll get. I'm especially susceptible to this in times of crisis. The adage "When the going gets tough, the tough get going," kicks in and, next thing I know, I'm working hard but not smart. Jon Acuff is clear: "The entrepreneur guru who tells you to work 80 hours a week is teaching you how to get a divorce, not how to be an entrepreneur."[5] The hard part of managing your time is staying accountable to a system. I need an accountability partner—not my spouse who loves me and will at times tolerate my self-deception—to keep me focused and committed. I've chosen my executive assistant, Faye Davis, to hold me to my commitments for each area of my calendar.

December is traditionally the slowest month for our businesses, so it's the perfect time to plan the next year, including my time allocation. Faye and I set aside two days to develop our plans—"our" because we work so closely together that my scheduling decisions affect her. We first review our existing commitments for the upcoming year and assign an estimated number of hours to achieve each one. We prioritize as follows:

1. Sleep and wellness
2. Holidays and vacations (family first!)
3. Commitments to my team members and the organization
4. Goals I've set with our board of directors
5. Commitments to outside boards
6. Speaking and creative writing
7. Personal development

Work-related time allotments assume fifty-two hours per week.

Next Faye and I create an Excel spreadsheet to visualize assigned or available blocks of time throughout the year. We follow a 70/20/10 formula—70 percent of time for the categories listed above, 20 percent reserved for new opportunities, and 10 percent for margin. Things happen. If I don't leave margin, I risk destruction of my ability to implement our mission. If I don't plan for unexpected time demands, they will eat into my missional responsibilities (the 70 percent), and I simply can't allow that. The Reverend Paul Rasmussen teaches, "We need to pre-decide what to do and what not to do when a moment of pressure arises."[6] I believe the saying "With no margin, there is no mission," and a 10 percent margin has proven adequate to enable me to accomplish the other 90 percent.

Now, this annual planning only works because Faye and I meet every few weeks to review the past few weeks. We then project ahead into the next month to ensure we will meet our internal and external commitments.

As a leader, I must manage my time strategically, based on my own rhythms, needs, and commitments, not as a scheduling prima donna. I have a family and fiduciary responsibility to maximize resources. When I said "I do" to Lyn twenty-nine years ago, I made a commitment to our family to be engaged and fully present. Equally important, when I accept leadership responsibility and compensation, I'm telling those depending on me that I will maximize my time, talents, and resources for them.

● ● ●

Beyond sleep, prayer and meditation, and time management, one key to keeping my leadership fully charged is understanding the rhythms of my commitments. Southwest Michigan First experiences two annual periods—April through June and September through November—when I can become overwhelmed if I don't remember that I just have to get to July 4 or Thanksgiving, respectively. I repeat a mantra ("Just make it to July 4") to remind myself, in the throes of the busy season, that it will end.

I also have to find healthy ways to achieve mental relaxation. Anticipating these high-stress seasons, I set aside novels by my favorite authors, and I allow myself to get lost in them, even if just for a few minutes at a time. I'm also a big believer in the power of moviegoing. Sitting in a dark, cool room, eating good popcorn, and disappearing in a great story almost always leave me feeling refreshed and refocused. Find something that allows you to push "pause" on your busy mind and allow that activity to refresh you.

Always take care to protect your joy. Leaders in any vocation can become so committed to their organizational mission that they forget to care for themselves. A high-performance car does no one any good sitting on the roadside with an empty tank.

ALWAYS FORWARD

- How might a commitment to starting your day with prayer or meditation (or both) change your life?
- Look at your calendar for the next ninety days. How could you apply a formula like my 70/20/10?

- If you allocate your time to what is most important, to what will you no longer be able to say yes? Or to what will you need to say yes less?
- Where are you at risk for burnout?
- What practices can you put into place to avoid or reverse these symptoms?

YOUR UNIQUE JOURNEY

If you need to protect or regain your joy, I encourage you to apply this chapter's lesson in your life and leadership. Or maybe your story wants to teach you something more important today. You could use pages 201–8 to mine life lessons from your unique journey.

19

What Do You Want?

AND OTHER QUESTIONS WE NEVER ANSWER

One reason so few of us achieve what we truly want is that we never direct our focus; we never concentrate our power. Most people dabble their way through life, never deciding to master anything too particular.

Tony Robbins

I love the movie *City Slickers*. In one scene the crusty cowboy, Curly (played by Jack Palance), tells the novice protagonist, Mitch Robbins (Billy Crystal), that there is only one secret to life—only one thing—and if you stick to that, everything else will fall into place. Robbins asks what the one thing is. The old cowboy replies, "That's what *you* have to find out."[1]

I see power in that advice. Libraries and bookstores are full of books about living your best life, chasing your dreams, organizing your time and space. But what does that all mean? I can name a dozen bestsellers about happiness from the last couple of years. But in truth most people never figure out what they really want. If you don't know what you want out of your life, you're not alone. A lot of us are taught that it's selfish to ask, "What do I want?"

In the early episodes of the television series *Scandal*, the main character, Olivia Pope, would ask her troubled clients, "What do you want? What do you want?" Like most of us, her clients could never seem to answer. They could describe their problem, but they couldn't define their desired outcome.

As you read this book, I hope you're gaining insight into parts of your life, figuring out what you want. What does your future hold? I challenge you to articulate your answers and write them down. Some may seem crazy, and that's okay. It's fine if you can't yet imagine how you will get there.

Early in my career I had the honor of working for a man who is still one of my heroes: United States Senator John Danforth. Senator Danforth is an incredible leader and a life-changing mentor to me. When I was working and traveling with him, we would go to grand homes that hosted his fundraisers. These involved dinner parties, and I was exposed to a level of quality and wealth I never knew existed. I never knew homes could be this spectacular, people could be this kind, and parties could be so charming. My concept of a party always included a keg of beer and barbecued chicken.

At this time Lyn and I were so broke, all we could afford were dreams. I had a mentor—a successful real estate broker—who consistently pushed me to talk with Lyn about

154

our hopes and dreams and write them down. I remember sitting with Lyn in our first apartment, four hundred square feet. It had a cramped combined kitchen/living room, one bedroom, and a bathroom so small we couldn't use the sink at the same time. We were at our two-person dining table discussing our dreams. This particular conversation occurred after a week attending fundraisers at amazing homes. I said, "Someday I want us to own a home so special that we could invite the governor and he would come."

She said, "We should write that down. That should be one of our goals."

You can see our first goal list, which came out of that conversation, in appendix B, as well as my current goal list in appendix C.

Many times, like Olivia Pope's clients or Mitch Robbins, we leaders don't know what we want—what we really want—so we end up describing our discontent. We know what we don't like—what we want to change or stop—but we don't know what will make us happy.

This past year Lyn and I were able to host the governor of Michigan at our lake home, Lyndon Hill, and I shared with the governor and other guests that they were witnessing the realization of a thirty-year dream. Following the event, two different guests, both of whom had helped facilitate our dream, approached me with the same comment: "Why didn't you say something earlier? You've always had a home nice enough to host the governor." I was too embarrassed to share my dream, so I nearly missed out on achieving it.

Things like this can only happen if you build your dreams in real time, not necessarily knowing how you're going to achieve them but believing that, if you jump, the net will

155

appear. And so, as you go about listening to your own life, I hope you do that for yourself.

ALWAYS FORWARD

- What do you want? What are ten things you want but have never had the courage to tell anyone?
- Who can help you achieve your dreams? What is holding you back from asking?

YOUR UNIQUE JOURNEY

You are welcome to apply this chapter's lesson in your life, or maybe your story wants to teach you something more important for this moment. On pages 201–8 I've provided a list of categories and prompts that might help you brainstorm and remember instructive stories and experiences.

20

The Kindness of Candor

HONESTY AS A GIFT WE GIVE

Candor is a compliment; it implies equality. It is
how true friends talk.

Peggy Noonan

When I started my leadership journey, it was commonly
believed that the point leader, on top of the pyramid,
should not associate with underlings but should be segre-
gated from them. Office buildings had private entrances and
elevators for management. A friend of mine, president of her
company, inherited such an office, along with a private rest-
room and private parking garage. She could go through an
entire day avoiding interaction with her team. (She doesn't,
by the way.) No wonder they used to say it was lonely at the
top. It was, by design.

Every time I see such an example of segregation, I'm reminded of the movie *Cool Hand Luke*. In one scene the

warden says, "What we have, here, is a failure to communicate."[1] The success of any organization depends on its team's commitment and output, and particularly on communication with each other. And that is best fostered by close proximity among the team. We spend a third of our lives with our fellow workers, and on an effective team our lives become inextricably interdependent. It's crazy to me that anyone would want to be isolated from their team.

Open communication between all positions is critical to successful organizations. Ed Catmull, cofounder of Pixar, states in his book *Creativity, Inc.* that "a company's communication structure should not mirror its organizational structure. Everybody should be able to talk to anybody."[2] A private elevator makes that hard.

Working closely with amazing people gives my leadership the high energy and creativity it requires. I need to absorb and be ignited by the fresh passion of emerging leaders, and this has nothing to do with anyone's title or role. Proximity also helps me see and assess the abilities of individuals to lead on their own.

Direct and open dialogue with your team encourages honesty and candor from them. One of my friends, the former president of a cereal company, once told me that, unless he is very intentional, "Information enters the building as Corn Flakes and gets to me as Frosted Flakes." Nobody wants to give the boss bad news, so if your team members don't trust you to accept their communications, they will put sweetener on them, mostly unconsciously. Personal and organizational success require that one important component of a trusting relationship—candor.

● ● ●

Let me tell you a little more about what I learned working for US Senator Jack Danforth, one of the finest people I've ever met. He is an Episcopal priest and has served as a state attorney general, senator, and US ambassador to the United Nations. Danforth is also a prolific mentor. His former staff include a Supreme Court justice, two US senators, members of Congress, and business and education leaders. One of the traits I admire in the senator is his commitment to candid feedback, delivered with love, with the goal of the recipient's growth.

For more than thirty years I have carried in my heart one talk with Jack after a campaign rally. At the last minute I had been asked to step in and introduce him to the crowd. I had often heard the standard Republican introduction: "We have to send Jack Danforth back to Washington to stop Ted Kennedy from ruining America." So this was how I introduced him.

After his speech we jumped in the car, and I prepared to drive him to the next stop. Before I could start the car, he asked me to wait. He then delivered a lesson, in loving candor, that I will never forget: "Thank you for jumping in and doing the introduction, but if you ever say what you said again, I will have to fire you. I cannot control what other people say or do, but I can direct what my team says. Ted Kennedy is a friend of mine, a great American, who loves this country as much as we do. I may disagree with him on some ideas, but we agree more than we disagree."

I was stunned and ashamed, but I also felt blessed that he would take time to teach me, not just discipline me. That was the day I learned a different way to conduct honest communication.

Honesty is never wrong, but its delivery can be hurtful and destructive. In thriving organizations, people know that candor is delivered for the best interest of all concerned, not to belittle someone. In order for honest conversations to be effective, they must be about ideas or actions, not people. Ed Catmull teaches his Pixar team, "You are not your idea. If you identify too closely with your ideas, you will take offense when your idea is challenged."[3] Pixar, the most successful studio of all time, was created with a priority on candor. When team members' work is criticized, they know they're not being attacked personally but rather others are trying to improve their idea and help them better serve their customers.

We on the giving side of candor must understand that it's cruel not to offer honest, forthright feedback and sometimes even discard an inferior idea. Lack of constructive openness is, in essence, stealing from the person and the group. Helpful criticism leads ultimately to great products that serve the needs of our market, our end users, or our congregation—people who count on us to be great.

It's easy for me, the point leader, to talk about candor because everybody loves the boss's ideas. Point leaders must be particularly careful to ensure their rank doesn't override the creative process, shutting down honesty from others. Receptiveness to candor must override hierarchy. Even though you are talented at organizational leadership, you must continually make clear that your ideas aren't necessarily best or final. Be intentional about creating environments where people can be honest. Seek out people willing to level with you and hold you accountable.

I was struck by the interaction Patrick Lencioni describes in his book *The Four Obsessions of an Extraordinary Executive*. His leadership team was duking it out over whether or not to take on a new project that had been presented to them.

Despite what anyone felt about the final decision, once it had been made, they all came on board with it. Constructive candor has a short memory. An effective team wholeheartedly supports a final decision.

Whether you are a marketplace, faith-based, or nonprofit leader, you owe it to your people—who get up every day and count on you to lead—to be as kindly candid as possible to produce outstanding products and service.

ALWAYS FORWARD

- Where have you seen candor delivered with kindness?
- What are the barriers to open communication on your team?
- How will you model and encourage constructive candor under your leadership?

YOUR UNIQUE JOURNEY

If you need this lesson about kind candor, please focus on this chapter's application in your life and leadership. Or feel free to let pages 201–8 help guide your exploration through your unique past experiences for a relevant life lesson for you.

21

Love Notes

TAKE A MINUTE, CHANGE A LIFE

Study after study shows there's no practice more
effective at increasing your happiness and well-
being than practicing radical gratitude.

Jud Wilhite

The first note I remember ever receiving was from my head
football coach on the Monday before the first game of my
senior year: "Congratulations. You will be our co-captain
Friday night. Your hard work, leadership, and character have
not gone unnoticed."

This meant the world to me. I felt honored, but this was
also the first time I was told I was a leader.

We can't rely on serendipity for opportunities to change
lives. Like my coach, we have to take initiative. At Southwest

Michigan First we choose to institutionalize appreciation; we regularly take time to lift each other up.

Oprah Winfrey said, "The more you praise and celebrate your life, the more there is in life to celebrate."[1] Southwest Michigan First takes this statement to heart, so we create ways every day to celebrate. We dedicate each Friday morning scrum meeting (see chapter 23) to sharing "Catalations" with each other. We coined this term by combining *catalyst*—a word we adopted at our founding to describe our core identity as catalysts of change—with *congratulation*. Catalations are written on a pad of flame-shaped notes. All team members use them to recognize each other, sharing words of affirmation or appreciation for something, great or small, a member has done during the week.

By the way, we also use Catalations to recognize the achievements of our many partner organizations, who help us accomplish our mission of job creation. We could not do it alone. To thank and celebrate them, we highlight community partners in our external communications and host luncheons on their behalf.

Lots of organizations put notes of affirmation on people's desks, but our public acknowledgment of each other's impact serves to lift the team up. Many leaders tell me they don't have time to write notes. I remind them that Doug Conant, former CEO of Campbell Soup, wrote thirty thousand notes in ten years while running one of America's greatest publicly traded companies.[2] That's an average of eleven notes per day for a decade!

We also like to celebrate the anniversaries of team members joining the organization. Other companies may give lapel pins or mention names in newsletters, but Southwest

you are a Catalyst

southwest michigan first

I believe in you

Michigan First asks every team member to write a note of specific appreciation to the celebrated person. On your anniversary, when you arrive at work, you find on your desk a fishbowl full of notes and a few other surprises. People share those notes at home, and I've heard from spouses what a powerful impact these affirmations have made.

Football fans don't wait until the end of the game to cheer. We applaud when players enter the field, when they exit, when they advance the ball, when they score points, when they fall down and get hurt, and when they get back up. But somehow we leaders forget to do that in the workplace. Gratitude and encouragement are more effective when they are immediate. Don't just think positive thoughts—that doesn't do any good. Tell them! When you see something great, pat your teammate on the back. Acknowledge small and great acts, in private and in front of their coworkers and supervisors.

This benefits you too. It's nearly impossible to lift others up and stay in a bad mood yourself. You know Jesus's teaching: "It is more blessed to give than to receive" (Acts 20:35). One of the best things I can do to de-stress myself is to write thank-you notes to others. I keep a notepad always sitting on my desk. When I don't have time to breathe, when my head is pounding and my inbox is full, I stop and write four or five notes. When I interrupt anxiety with gratitude, I inevitably feel better and become more productive, so I can make up the time the notes required. Sure, my notes lift up others, but they also serve my enlightened self-interest, reenergizing me and my leadership.

Janet Comenos, cofounder of Spotted, maintains a list of people who helped her start and grow her company. Each morning she sends one of these people a text or email of thanks, sharing about how business is going, what she's learning, or information that might benefit them. I wish I was on Janet's list.

When I travel and find myself with extra time, you can find me either at a great local bookstore (I've been known to buy another suitcase to get my purchases home) or at a restaurant led by a creative chef or restaurateur (yes, I stalk everyone on Bravo's *Top Chef*). I recently planned to eat at Union Square Café in New York City, led by Danny Meyer of Shake Shack fame. When I make reservations, I always ask to meet the chef or owner and give him or her my regards. This time I also asked, if possible, to purchase a signed copy of Meyer's book *Setting the Table*. A few days early, Meyer called to apologize that he would not be in the restaurant that day. He thanked me for coming and said a signed book would await my arrival. Talk about a "note" of appreciation!

If you really want to take your leadership to the next level, try sending a note congratulating your competition when they best you. I'm impressed by the dynamic leadership of Taylor Swift when she sent Cardi B flowers and a note congratulating her for earning number one on *Billboard*'s Hot 100 Chart and knocking Taylor's song down to number two.[3] I'll bet Cardi B never forgets Swift's kindness and class.

Tom Peters, author of *In Search of Excellence,* shared on Twitter that since 1973 he has used New Year's week to call twenty-five to fifty people and thank them for their support over the past year.[4]

It's my semiannual tradition to set aside time to contemplate the past six months. I look back on my decisions and the people who influenced them. Then I write each person a

I CANNOT IMAGINE WHAT WE WOULD BE WITHOUT YOU. THANK YOU FOR CHOOSING US EVERY DAY! - RON

note thanking them for the difference they made in my life, sharing as much detail as possible about the decision and their influence. Occasionally I get a thank-you in response, but that's not why I do it. Expressing my thanks is good for me. A study published by *Psychotherapy Research* reported that gratitude-writing participants "reported significantly better mental health" than other participants in the study.[5]

Not long ago I received an unexpected note: "Ron, in 1983 you gave me a tank of gas that allowed me to get home to northwest Missouri. That tank of gas was a turning point in my life. I will never forget it." I remembered its writer, Randy. He was in a band with some friends of mine, but, to be honest, I don't remember that tank of gas. But whatever it cost me was inconsequential compared to the value of that note. On the tough days, when I'm feeling down, overwhelmed, underappreciated, or just off my game, I pull out Randy's note and others like it, or Catalations from my team, to remind me of my "why" and recharge my leadership.

● ● ●

You may never know what lasting imprint you might make on another's life. What may seem like a passing encounter can change someone's course for good. Just make sure your impact is positive. Joel Manby, former CEO of SeaWorld Parks and Entertainment, is from the Kalamazoo area and became semifamous after his appearance on the first season of *Undercover Boss*. He once told me about a time a small gesture made a profound difference for him. Early in his career he received an offer from a competitor to work for them. They offered a much more distinguished position and far higher pay. Joel was seriously considering the offer when his current boss, unaware that Joel was considering leaving, sent a personal note home to Joel's family that read something like this: "I wish you could see your dad and husband at work. Every day he is changing the lives of our guests, but also the lives of the people he works alongside. He does incredible work, and we are so lucky to have him with us. I want to thank you for the sacrifice your family makes by letting him spend time with us."

When he and his wife read that letter, his wife said, "You could never leave this company. There is no place we could go where they would love our family the way this letter showed love to our family." I try to follow that leader's example and have made a practice of writing similar letters to our team's family members.

A simple show of appreciation through a note or a small gift will help you retain quality contacts. Dr. Gary Chapman, author of *The Five Love Languages*, reports that "64 percent of Americans who leave their jobs say they do so because they don't feel appreciated."[6] According to a 2004 Maritz poll, "81 percent of respondents who had never received a 'Thank You' from a superior for a job well-done said they were very likely to leave their current job."[7]

Poet William James summarizes the importance of expressing appreciation in *The Principles of Psychology*:

> No more fiendish punishment could be devised, were such a thing physically possible, than that one should be turned loose in society and remain absolutely unnoticed by all the members thereof. If no one turned round when we entered, answered when we spoke, or minded what we did, but if every person we met "cut us dead," and acted as if we were non-existing things, a kind of rage and impotent despair would ere long well up in us, from which the cruelest bodily tortures would be a relief.[8]

A few years ago we were interviewing a senior leader to join our team. I happened to know the candidate well, and we shared great trust. I knew she'd been transparent with her current employer about this interview, but what happened on day two of her visit with us surprised and impressed me. That morning she received from the chair of her board a FedEx package containing a hardcover book of clippings about her successes as their leader, as well as notes from board members, community leaders, and elected officials (including the governor), telling her how much they loved her and asking her to stay. With the book was a letter to me stating that, if she decided to stay with them, they would reimburse my expenses. In case she joined our team, they provided quotes for our press release, praising and encouraging her.

I got my money back.

Exceptional leaders allow themselves to be vulnerable and are willing to go above and beyond to engage with their people. It may feel uncomfortable at times to humble yourself or express profound gratitude, but respect and dedication is a two-way street.

King David wrote, "I will give thanks to You forever," and "I will praise You with my whole heart" (Ps. 30:12; 138:1 NKJV). Gratitude has been vital to our souls since inception.

ALWAYS FORWARD

- When have you received a note of gratitude? How did it make you feel?
- Whose joy can you take to the next level by sending them a note?
- What practices of regular gratitude could you institute in your organization?

YOUR UNIQUE JOURNEY

Feel free to apply my love notes lesson in your life and leadership, or maybe your unique life story offers an even more important lesson for this point in your journey. Pages 201–8 might help.

22

Preeminence

DEFINING YOUR STANDARDS

Excellence is no longer an option, nor does it happen by accident. Excellence is a matter of understanding who you are as a person, an organization, a family—it's knowing what matters to you.

Ron Kitchens

I wrote *Uniquely You* for the individual seeking to embrace personal life stories to chart his or her life, but I've also been asked how these principles translate into organizational authenticity and excellence. So I'm offering here a description of one of our practices, which we call "preeminence."

It's the leader's job to be clear about the organization's nonnegotiable core values. They are the riverbanks that help guide and refine the team. Lack of riverbanks creates a swamp, which might make for interesting reality television, but the loss of navigability and water clarity kills opportunity and growth.

My ongoing study of excellence has led to this book and has started Southwest Michigan First on the path to becoming preeminent. I never wanted our organization to be like a sports team that wins one season, never to be heard from again. I live in fear that I might grow complacent as a leader and allow our team to become simply average. Average is one stop away from irrelevant, risking my fellow workers' financial and professional lives and crippling our mission and impact.

In describing our drive for achievement, terms like *elite*, *world class*, and *best of the best* don't fully capture its essence. For us the word *preeminence* best sums up what we hope to achieve. To the world *preeminence* is a noun—a state or character of being preeminent. In our culture it's more: preeminence means extraordinary excellence that, once reached and sustained, creates a lasting and competitive advantage.

Note two key words in our definition—*reached* and *sustained*. Any sports team can get lucky and win a single championship. Similarly, weak organizations can get lucky and have a great quarter. It's therefore critical to plot a course carefully, rising above luck to reach and sustain extraordinary excellence.

The goal is not simply excellence but *extraordinary* excellence. Basic excellence is expected in today's marketplace, our societal standard. If you do something incredible this week, it becomes the expectation next week. When we enter a business, we expect the highest level of service we've ever experienced, and on our next visit we'll expect the same or better. Chick-fil-A is a splendid example. Why does Chick-fil-A, which is open fewer hours, sell four times as much food per store as McDonald's? They deliver on excellence—sustained levels of excellence—in quality of customer experience.

172

Our Organizational Axioms

It's not enough to say simply, "We want to be great." Preeminent teams must understand how to meet expectations day to day to reach and sustain greatness. Southwest Michigan First has developed thirteen axioms that define our journey. Your axioms or verbiage will undoubtedly be different, but, I wager, not substantially different.

Axiom 1: Different by Design

We choose our own path. We're simply not willing to let a status quo mentality define success for us. How much different would our nation be if Howard Schultz of Starbucks had listened to naysayers who didn't believe people wanted a better cup of coffee?

Axiom 2: Curate the Future

This is about deciding what and who you intend to be. An organizational leader's single most important objective is to clarify a vision of the future, answering the question, What will the future look like? Great organizations don't let others or outside conditions determine their future; they chart their own futures.

Axiom 3: Boundless Curiosity

Great leaders are hungry for knowledge and terrified of missing the next wave of change. This curiosity, which drives us to be "in the know," is the key to an organization's ability to stay ahead of competitors and exceed its customers' expectations.

One of my favorite activities when I travel is to find a bookstore and buy an armload of magazines I've never seen before. I want to know how other industries think. What are they talking about? What design aesthetic is important to them? What do they take for granted that I should know? When leaders lose their curiosity, they become stale and lose their right to lead.

Axiom 4: Challenge and Change Our Best Every Day

In a world where nearly every song ever recorded, every book ever written, and every movie ever produced is available instantly on your phone, you can't expect your work to remain a secret. To your customers, your best today represents their minimum expectation tomorrow, and, with competitors ready to replicate your successful methods, the only way to thrive beyond today is to reinvent your future every day.

A tremendous example of reinvention is Netflix. Over the years the company has transitioned from a mail-order DVD service to an online streaming hub to its current position as a prominent content creator garnering 112 Emmy nominations in 2018. Netflix is always changing its best.

Axiom 5: Process Creates Outcomes

Great leaders understand that, in a world of automation and instant access, they can't afford to have all decisions made at the top; they must transfer responsibility to levels closer to the customer. To achieve lower-level decision making, processes must be in place to ensure that everyone in the organization has the knowledge and development essentials for making good decisions.

Axiom 6: Never Cheat

You might think this is a given, but it's not. I mean *never* cheat. Never cheat on your expense account. Never cheat on your taxes. Never cheat at your golf game. Never cheat paying for parking. Never cheat. Why? If you can't be trusted to do the easy things honestly, how can you ever be trusted to lead?

Axiom 7: Transparent Relationships

This could easily be called the "no gossip" rule, but it goes further than that. People today are hungry for authentic relationships that go beyond the old nine-to-five paradigm. Today all areas of our lives are integrated, and people want that same connection at work. When you want your coworkers to understand your hopes and dreams and they want you to understand theirs, you can easily collaborate and find success together.

Axiom 8: Diversity Reflects Destiny

My doctor reminds me during every annual physical, "You are what you eat." For organizations, that sage wisdom can be translated, "Diversity reflects destiny." A diversity of ideas, backgrounds, genders, races, and educations—you get the idea—brings strength, knowledge, and capacity to elevate and accelerate your organization.

Axiom 9: We Are Guides, Coaches, and Consultants

I remember well the first time I heard someone say, "That's not my job." I told myself I never wanted to work anywhere that tolerates those words. Our role in any situation is determined by those we're serving, not our titles, egos, or positions on an organizational chart.

Axiom 10: CEO of Your Own Responsibilities

Each of us has an obligation to manage our responsibilities to the best of our abilities and to be good stewards of our resources. Great organizations take this philosophy to the next level. They not only set lofty expectations but they give everyone the same freedom as the CEO for deciding how and when they work. Great organizations empower and trust everyone.

Axiom 11: Servers, Not Guests

Servant leadership is critically important, but too many people embrace the leadership role and forget the servant part. We never want to act like guests. No matter the situation, we always strive to serve those around us. The simple things like walking across the room to speak to someone who seems isolated at an event, thanking a staff person for making your experience wonderful, or just sharing a smile with someone you pass in the hall are important. When you care more about others' comfort than your own, you find true grace and greatness.

Axiom 12: Live as Examples

Every major religion in the world holds the same basic tenet: "Love thy neighbor." With so much agreement, it would seem a simple concept for us all to embrace. Sadly, this is not true. At Southwest Michigan First we believe we have a responsibility to live as examples of love and respect for our customers and coworkers. We hold ourselves to standards that are hard to achieve but imperative if we want to curate a better world.

Axiom 13: Family First

This axiom used to be worded "choosing to cheat" after the Andy Stanley book, but since axiom 6 says, "Never cheat," this one needed new wording. The concept is simple: whatever job you do today will someday be done by someone else. The only exception is your place in your family; only you can fulfill that role. At some point you will have to decide between family or work, and we make that choice easy: family. Our team is expected to attend their children's events, stay home when they're sick, and fully embrace their family commitments.

It's critical that we leaders not only *support* "family first," but *live* it as well. One rule at PepsiCo Australia and New Zealand is "Leave loudly." Leaders are expected to take care of their families and their health, making sure that everyone knows they're doing so by announcing when they leave early and sharing why. Teams will follow the behaviors modeled by their leaders. Thus it is critical that leaders leave loudly.

My Personal Axioms

Commitment to a life of preeminence is not just important in order for organizations, groups, and teams to thrive; the individual also must be personally committed to this journey. My personal preeminence axioms serve as my north star to ensure I'm moving forward and living an intentional life.

Axiom 1: Stay on the Wall

I've adopted as my life verse Nehemiah 6:3, which seems to me the cornerstone of Nehemiah's story. Nehemiah, responding to those who would distract him from his mission, said, "I am doing a great work and I cannot come down. Why should the work stop while I leave it and come down to you?" Create a plan, define its outcomes and time frame, and execute it. Don't pay attention to what others are doing; they're not running your race.

Axiom 2: Curate the People in Your Life

You can't serve everyone, nor does everyone need you. Surround yourself with those who want to be preeminent in their lives, who make you a better, happier, wiser person.

Axiom 3: Live as If You Need a Hundred Pallbearers

Share knowledge, relationships, and resources.

Axiom 4: You Are the Only Person Called to Be Kelsey's Dad and Lyn's Husband

Act accordingly.

Axiom 5: You Are Not an Accident; You're Here for a Purpose

Playing small or underperforming is an insult to God. Remember, it was the guy who buried his talents that Christ condemned (see Matt. 25:14–30).

Axiom 6: If You're Not Learning, You're Dying

ABL: Always be learning.

Axiom 7: Annually Master Something Hard and Lonely

Each year attempt and master something that takes individual work and concentration, something you have to do by yourself, something no one else can do for you.

Axiom 8: Always Forward

When you are stuck and don't know what to do, keep going forward. Your future is in that direction.

The Journey

Preeminence is a journey that's never complete. It's always a race in progress with a moving finish line, but the journey is worth the effort. In a world of high expectations, cost pressures, and scarcity of talent, the only way to thrive is by ensuring your organization is the best of the best.

The confidence from living a life of preeminence is truly liberating. Once you define excellence for yourself, "average" will never again satisfy your expectations.

ALWAYS FORWARD

- What axioms define you personally?
- What changes in your life do you need to make to be preeminent?
- What would your perfect preeminent organization look like?

YOUR UNIQUE JOURNEY

You are welcome to apply my preeminence lesson in your life, or maybe your story wants to teach you something more important for this moment. On pages 201–8 I've provided a list of categories and prompts that might help you brainstorm and remember instructive stories and experiences.

23

Scrum

GATHERING FOR IMPACT

> Never doubt that a small group of thoughtful,
> committed citizens can change the world; indeed,
> it's the only thing that ever has.
>
> Margaret Mead

In a time when consumers are savvy and cautious, how do you add lagniappe in your business? How do you provide that little extra that binds your customers to your company? How do you create raving fans, not casual consumers?

For many years I played rugby. It's a passionate game, full of action and requiring teamwork and perseverance. The goal of rugby is similar to that of football; to score, your team must get the ball across the try (goal) line.

I played the position of loose head prop, which is among the forwards. The forwards form the scrum—the huddle-like formation that is the most recognizable rugby image. The scrum is said to resemble two rams coming together in a violent collision. The purpose of the scrum is like that of a jump ball in basketball—to restart game play.

Forwards are also equivalent to linemen in football; they do the hard physical work. But most often they must give the ball to the backs to score, and the backs receive the cheers and glory. The backs are usually the beautiful players whose uniforms stay clean and fresh smelling—who look like Diana Ross at her famous Central Park concert, hair blowing in the wind. (Okay, I might be slightly bitter.)

The scrum is a great metaphor for teams of servant leaders. We must do the hard work, understanding that, regardless of who gets the recognition, we win as a team.

At Southwest Michigan First our entire team of thirty or so gets together each morning at 8:05 for scrum (so don't call at that time; we won't answer). As in a rugby match, we meet to discuss how we're going to move always forward throughout the days and weeks for our organization's success.

Each team member's role is to get in and do the hard, grinding work, but to score, often they will have to pass the ball to someone else who will cross the line and gain the glory. But it's really not about who gets the glory. What matters most is working together as a team, doing the challenging work, and knowing that, when the ball crosses the line, we all win. So during our morning scrum we decide who is the best person to carry the ball that day for any given task.

Our scrum meetings have a rhythm that focuses on internal communication, team engagement, and mission acceleration. We use the following to ensure we stay on task. Each month the team elects the scrum's Legacy Leader for that month—similar to other organizations' employee of the month, but we require our team to select by asking, "Who will leave their lasting imprint, or legacy, on the organization?"

Scrum Schedule

Monday—Open Calendars

Every member shares relevent elements of their calendar for the week, focusing on areas where team insights would benefit them and information they have that might benefit others.

Tuesday—Vision Cast

A senior member, usually the CEO or someone responsible for kicking off a new initiative, spends ten to fifteen minutes speaking about direction and focus. Vision is critical, and communicating that vision is key. The team can depend for a while on my understanding of the organization's vision, but eventually they all must clearly understand it so that team members can mature by aligning their individual visions to the organization's.

Wednesday—Marketing and Customer Service Stories

Each team member shares either a customer service experience or a positive or negative example of marketing, sales, or advertising. Usually examples are either innovative or somehow telling and help us examine our practices.

Thursday—Data (Every Other Week)

We track our numbers on a scoreboard that resembles the famed Wrigley Field scoreboard. On it we also record our team's specific strategies and tactical goals. Reviewing our numbers allows a discussion about best ways to achieve our goals and clarifies where we may be falling behind.

Thursday—Insight (Every Other Week)

We engage in exercises to share information about ourselves and our lives to deepen our relationships. We may ask about favorite songs, favorite foods, or our dream jobs when we were thirteen.

Friday—Catalations

I've previously described our Catalations—a term that merges *catalyst* and *congratulation*. Team members exchange these notes of appreciation, recognizing commitment, engagement, and collaboration, as well as milestones in a member's leadership.

Each day our scrum focuses on a topic that will strategically move the organization forward. Scrums are often exercises in creativity, in which we learn what each team member finds inspiring, how uniquely we each answer the same question, and how funny each of us can be. What better way to start each workday than in awe of the individual perspective, thoughts, and gifts of each teammate?

Maybe you still doubt that scrums, or something like them, are worth the cost of everyone's time. Or maybe you would love to start them but need to convince your boss of their worth. Robert Orben said, "If you think education is expensive, try ignorance."[1] That's really what our morning meetings are about. If you think meeting together as a team is expensive, consider the cost of not doing it. We save much time because our meetings help us avoid replicated effort, ensure clarity of communication, and constantly reinforce our culture.

The effect also shows in our success metrics: our turnover is far lower than industry standards, and our productivity is far higher. I can't imagine ever being part of an organization that didn't meet once a day to rebalance, recharge, and re-imagine itself. These are realities that should convince you or your leadership.

ALWAYS FORWARD

- How are you ensuring your team is all-in on your culture?
- What is holding you back from your own version of the daily scrum?
- What will you do each day?

YOUR UNIQUE JOURNEY

It might be a high priority for you to implement something like scrums in your life and leadership. But if your life story is trying to teach you something more important, feel free to explore your unique journey, perhaps using pages 201–8.

24

The Four Most Powerful Words

"I BELIEVE IN YOU"

> Piglet noticed that even though he had a Very
> Small Heart, it could hold a rather large amount
> of Gratitude.
>
> A. A. Milne

I believe in you.
I believe in you.
I believe in you.

Those are the four most powerful words in a leader's vocabulary. These words have been the Miracle Gro for my life and leadership journey. The belief of others was often the fuel that propelled me when I had no idea where I was going or even what I wanted.

Established leaders, I encourage you to become agents of "I believe in you," to pour into emerging leaders as though

186

your future depends on it. It probably does. Your belief in those you lead can start small, as Mark Batterson shares in *Chase the Lion*:

> Every decision we make, every risk we take, has a chain reaction. And those chain reactions set off a thousand chain reactions we aren't even aware of. The cumulative effect won't be revealed until we reach the other side of the space-time continuum.
>
> It takes very little effort to push over a tiny domino, only .024 joules of input energy. You can do it with your pinky finger. By the time you reach the thirteenth domino, the gravitational potential energy is two billion times greater than the energy it took to knock over that first domino. My point? Some of us want to start with the Leaning Tower of Pisa or the Eiffel Tower or the Empire State Building. Good luck with that.[1]

The Japanese have a word, *kaizen*. It means change that leads to constant improvement. If you are reading this, you too are practicing *kaizen*, seeking excellence but understanding that great organizations change and improve their best every day. Adapt. Grow. Replenish.

Emerging leaders, I believe in you.

I believe the world's future is bright because of your passion. Focus on mission, equity, and excellence. Don't let the world tell you that you need to wait to lead; you have all the world's knowledge literally at your fingertips. But it's not mere knowledge that will make you great, impactful, or influential. It's understanding how to use that knowledge.

This book was written as a road map to help you see how your unique experiences, if you listen to them, will give you the discernment to transform your leadership, becoming the leader only you can be.

ALWAYS FORWARD

- Who can you reach out to today to tell them that you believe in them?
- When in your life has the power of someone's belief in you propelled your leadership?

YOUR UNIQUE JOURNEY

You are welcome to apply my lesson about the four most powerful words, or maybe your story wants to teach you something more important for this moment. On pages 201–8 I've provided a list of categories and prompts that might help you brainstorm and remember instructive stories and experiences.

00

I'm Glad You Asked

A FEW MORE THOUGHTS

Over the past decade I've created blogs, podcasts, and TV programs and spoken to tens of thousands of leaders. I've received more questions than I can count—by email, text, and phone—about how to be a unique leader while learning from others. Here I've resurrected some of those questions and offered my latest thoughts.

Our Team Is in a Rut

Question: Our team feels stuck after a season of abundance. Have you experienced this? What are your suggestions for jump-starting the team?

Answer: Southwest Michigan First believes in a system we call LEAP—Laugh, Exercise, Art, and Praise. When we're in

189

the doldrums and need to recharge our leadership, we bring the entire team together for a day to LEAP.

First, "Laughter is the best medicine" always proves true for our team. If we can laugh together during the day—or any time—the stress and tension visibly melt away.

Second, we usually use part of our day exercising in competitive activities, such as our annual kickball classic—which incorporates a generous amount of trash talking—or water sports. Our exercise sometimes includes our team members' many small children.

Third, we use part of our team day to produce art, although calling some of our creations art might be an exaggeration. Together we craft something to display in our offices—like the glass construction we kiln fired, the painting that included each team member's thumbprint, and the metal version of our logo that we built while learning to be blacksmiths.

And fourth, as the point leader, I facilitate the praise portion of the day. I might publicly praise team members for their impact, or team members might share what they enjoy about each other.

I hope our LEAP model, or something like it, helps you out of your rut. It always seems to do it for us.

Are We Growing Too Fast?

Question: Our company is growing tremendously, and I'm worried we'll grow too fast. I've heard you say, "More companies die of indigestion than starvation"—that is, an abundance of opportunities can cause companies to lose focus, rather than focusing on a few choice opportunities. How have you handled Southwest Michigan First's growth? How have you prevented "death by indigestion"?

Answer: I can understand your concerns. Over the last thirteen years Southwest Michigan First has seen double-digit annual growth, averaging nearly 20 percent. In the early years I too worried that growth would cause loss of culture or our systems would fail. Some of this did happen, but it caused change for the better. By getting bigger, we gained scale, which enabled achievements with highly talented people that we wouldn't otherwise have reached. All living organisms must grow to thrive, and your organization is living. If you're not growing, you're dying.

Growing pains are real, as is the fear they instill. But if you focus on communication, understand the nonnegotiable areas of your culture, and maintain a strong sense of adventure, you will weather this storm and come out with greater impact and influence.

Getting My Life Back

Question: People constantly bombard me with requests for my time that aren't part of my job responsibility, and I feel guilty saying no. I end up spending my day in meetings that don't benefit my company, then using nights and weekends for my real work. My company, my family, and I all lose. How can I manage these requests?

Answer: I also struggle to say no, and I always will. I love to help people solve problems. But I can't "steal" from my company, my family, or my health.

191

I budget my time just as I budget my money. As with my household budget, I can't spend what I don't have. I can find ways to make more money, but I can do nothing to create more time, so I have to learn to tell people no, even if it never feels comfortable. I try to do it nicely, but I remind them I've committed that time, and if I were to give it to them, I would have to disappoint somebody else.

My integrity is worth a lot, so I must turn down most extra opportunities. Nehemiah 6:3 reminds me to stay consistently on my wall, doing the work to which I've committed. I can seldom come down and fulfill other requests. I encourage you to focus on that. I also recommend the book *Essentialism* by Greg McKeown. It offers valuable tips for managing your time without feeling guilty.

Mentors for the Mentor

Question: You've told about designating Millennials as your accountability partners and giving them responsibility to wave a red flag when you're not being relevant or to coach you through new technologies or cultural changes. How can I encourage that same kind of coaching relationship with a young team member?

Answer: First, choose somebody you believe has high potential, who will become a better leader when you lift them up and give them exposure to new opportunities with you. Second, choose someone with loads of confidence, who is a natural teacher. You, the boss, are not going to be an easy student.

As you embark on this journey, I recommend that you make specific requests, such as, "I'd love for you to teach me about X." Then set aside the time you truly need and devote it fully to learning together. You can't be on your phone the whole time. You can't be in CEO-I'm-important mode. You must be a student, ready to learn. Once you've reinforced that pattern several times, you'll find the trust in those mentoring sessions beginning to spill over into other aspects of your working relationship.

I've had that relationship with several team members. A couple have gone on to lead their own organizations, and I still receive feedback from them: "Hey, here's something I think you'd want to know about, something you'd want to learn, a conference you ought to attend. Here's a quote that reminded me of you." But you must pursue this intentionally, and both parties must make it a high priority. You must make sure your next-generation mentor knows they have permission to teach you or give honest feedback. And it's a formal relationship, not just, "Hey, let's hang out, and tell me cool things."

Who Do I Know?

Question: I deeply desire to learn from leaders to whom I don't have ready access. How can I get meetings with these men and women?

Answer: I have been exactly where you are, and the advice I received has served me well. Remember these people are busy, so don't expect them to say yes unless you send a compelling message. While you may not have direct access, it's worth checking with people you know who do have access to the person. Seek out databases that show connections among board members, looking for people you know who would be able and willing to introduce you. Attend conferences where your target leader is speaking. Unless they're ultra VIP, they're usually more than pleased to meet fans, and you can then ask for a future meeting.

Nearly a hundred times, with good success, I've sent an email or letter requesting thirty minutes to ask three specific questions on leadership. I offer, as a token of my appreciation, a donation in their name to a charity of their choice. I can only remember three occasions when this didn't work, and in each of those the CEO left the company within a month.

One caveat: don't waste the meeting time praising them. Have your questions ready, and stick to the time limit. For what it's worth, my third question is always one that John Maxwell shared when I spoke with him: "Whom do you know that I should know, and will you introduce me to them?"

● ● ●

I hope these ideas have been helpful. If you have other questions, please email me at ron@ronkitchens.com, message me on Facebook, or use any communication method you prefer. I'd be tickled to death to share my thoughts.

Always forward.

When one man, for whatever reason, has the opportunity to lead an extraordinary life, he has no right to keep it to himself.

Jacques-Yves Cousteau

In Summary

PRINCIPLES FROM MY LIFE STORY

Here are key principles from the stories I've shared from my past. I hope this will serve you as a quick reference after you've finished this book.

Chapter 0 *Changed for Good*

Listen to your life; put into practice the lessons your story is trying to teach you.

Chapter 1 *Mandarin Oranges*

Never minimize the importance of small kindnesses; offer them often and see lives change.

Chapter 2 *"You Can't Read"*

Never stop learning—especially from great books—in order to broaden yourself and enhance your leadership effectiveness.

Chapter 3 *Lunch Shaming*

Choose solutions that are more than merely expedient—solutions that respect people and lift them up.

Chapter 4 *Pork Chops*

Observe successful people; learn and live from what you see.

Chapter 5 *Legacy*

Live and lead now with a view toward the impact you will leave on people after you're gone.

Chapter 6 *"I Know You Can"*

Help others see their future by forecasting it with optimism. Show them you believe in them!

Chapter 7 *Lagniappe*

Enhance your reputation and quality of service by adding that little something extra.

Chapter 8 *"Let Me Predict Your Future"*

Welcome the input of people who love you enough to tell you the hard truth.

Chapter 9 *"That's Not Our Plan"*

Once your dream has become clear, stay the course, resisting distractions.

Chapter 10 *The Four Horses*

Seek to understand yourself and pursue the race you were created to run.

Chapter 11 *Great Teams*

Organizations and teams benefit from members who are different from the rest.

Chapter 12 *Surround Yourself*

Strategically choose a circle of influencers in your life who will make you better.

Chapter 13 *No Fences*

Where you can, challenge injustice and knock down artificial barriers between people groups.

Chapter 14 *CEO of Your Own Responsibilities*

In every aspect of your work, large and small, serve and lead as if you were the owner; give your team members this same freedom and challenge.

Chapter 15 *Family First*

Give priority to your most important job—the loved ones in your care.

Chapter 16 *Be Original*

Living with authenticity and integrity, inspiring others, and building your brand will help you achieve leadership impact.

Chapter 17 *Action over Emotion*

Conquer fears—real and imagined—by taking responsible action to minimize or eliminate the feared outcomes.

Chapter 18 *Protecting Joy*

Seek out people, environments, and intellectual "food" that move you toward excellence; edit out all that don't.

Chapter 19 *What Do You Want?*

Take the time and make the effort to achieve clarity about your important life goals and how to achieve them.

Chapter 20 *The Kindness of Candor*

Help your people grow by telling them the truth constructively, cushioned in compassion.

Chapter 21 *Love Notes*

A short note of encouragement can change a life; make written affirmation a regular feature of your leadership practice.

Chapter 22 *Preeminence*

Carefully choose, define, communicate, and support your organizational standards.

Chapter 23 *Scrum*

Implement frequent team gatherings to enhance organizational efficiency and impact.

Chapter 24 *The Four Most Powerful Words*

Demonstrate to others that you believe in them.

Mining Lessons
from Your Unique Life Story

Following are a number of different approaches to exploring your unique life experience from different angles, through different lenses. You might find that one approach helps you remember only so many instructive experiences. A different angle might turn up other memories. Some of your stories might require time to remember, so keep coming back and trying again from time to time as you read through this book. Some of my stories and "Always Forward" questions might also trigger memories from your unique experience.

When you remember a story from your life, in order to let it teach you its lessons, follow a two-step pattern:

1. Explore and record the important *details* of the story. Who was involved? What happened? What choices did you or others make? How did it turn out? How did this experience impact and change you long-term?

2. What life *lesson* did that experience teach? Did you learn the lesson then? Later? Ever? Have other experiences reinforced the same lesson over time? How can you apply that lesson in your present and future? In your personal life? In your leadership at work or elsewhere?

You might compile several stories in one sitting or one or two at a time. Once you've finished this book, I urge you to establish a habit of regularly recording additional stories and their lessons as they come to mind.

Once you've gathered a number of stories and their lessons, you might wish to find a way to sort them by priority. Which lessons require your most immediate attention and application in your life and leadership? Give each story/lesson a title, list the titles, then rearrange them in priority order. You might attach target progress or completion dates for goals that arise from your stories and what they teach.

Exploring through Questions

Choose one (at a time) of these questions to help you brainstorm stories from your life experience.

- Imagine you are sitting around a fire with your most trusted friends. The night grows long, and you feel free to be honest and transparent. You know any story you share will never be repeated. Which tales would you tell? How would your friends react? Now pause. How can you use these stories to shape your leadership?
- If you comprised a highlight reel of your life, which stories would you include?

202

- What in your past experiences has come to define your leadership? How can you use this to strengthen your organization?
- Which experiences in your life have become your hardened, protective shell? Are they like a knight's armor that expands with your movement, or are they rigid and inflexible, restricting your growth?
- What issue or issues from your past were formative? If they influenced you positively, how will you build on them now? If they influenced you negatively, how can you work to remediate or eliminate their effect? How would you summarize their lessons?

Exploring Your Life Seasons

One way to remember your life experiences is to picture different phases of your life.

- Your preschool years (birth–age 5)
- Your childhood (ages 6–12)
- Your teens (ages 13–18)
- Your young adulthood (ages 19–30)
- Your middle years (ages 30–50)
- Your later years (age 50+)

Exploring Areas of Life

Some of your life stories might come to mind by thinking about life's different arenas of experience.

203

- Your family of origin
- Your marriage and family
- Friends
- Physical health
- Intellectual growth
- Spirituality
- Political, economic, and social issues
- Community connections
- Conflicts and hardships
- Happy times
- Character qualities
- Personality
- Purpose in life
- Your routines and what they reveal

Exploring Leadership Topics

Pondering some of these leadership issues might help you remember some of your instructive life stories and their lessons.

- *Integrity and honesty.* When did you see or experience the value or cost of honesty in leadership? Of dishonesty? Tell about the time you first realized the importance of personal integrity.
- *Commitment, reliability.* Tell a story about a time you enjoyed the reward of commitment, or when you or someone paid the cost of being unreliable.
- *Resiliency through adversity.* Recall a story in which you or someone you know learned to endure through

great difficulty. What principles have your experiences taught you for coming back stronger after a setback?

- *Creativity.* When have you or someone you know seen the value of creative thinking to find solutions that otherwise remained undiscovered? What made this creativity possible?

- *Relationships.* Tell a story about a relationship that was instrumental in your leadership success or growth. Tell about your most important relationships. What have your experiences taught you about building and sustaining valuable relationships?

- *Teams.* Tell about a time when people working together accomplished something that would otherwise have been impossible or of lesser quality. What methods do your life stories teach you for improving teamwork?

- *Leadership and followership.* When have you seen or practiced effective or ineffective leadership? Effective or ineffective followership? What principles have your experiences taught you about the impact of leaders on followers, and vice versa?

- *Success, failure, and mistakes.* Tell about one of your successes (or that of someone you know) and what it taught you. Tell about one of your (or another's) failures or mistakes and what you learned from it.

- *Strengths and weaknesses.* What were the circumstances in which you first discovered one of your strengths or weaknesses? Tell a story in which one of your strengths or weaknesses played a significant role. How have these experiences contributed to your philosophy for making the most of self-knowledge?

- *Experience, learning, and wisdom.* Tell about a time when you or someone you know benefited from past experience, learning, or acquired wisdom. What have your life stories taught you about best practices for acquiring experience, learning, and wisdom?
- *Self-care.* Describe circumstances in which you learned the importance of self-care. What areas and methods for self-care have you derived from your life experience?
- *Generosity and caring for others.* Tell a story in which you saw or practiced generosity or care for others (or when these were withheld or someone was mistreated).
- *Motivation, encouragement.* When did you discover the importance of motivation and encouragement in leadership? What have your experiences taught you about the ways you are best motivated? About best practices for motivating and uplifting others?
- *Vision, direction.* Tell about an experience in which you saw the value of leadership vision and direction. What principles for implementing vision and direction have you gained from your life stories?

Exploring Stories People Tell about You

We need other people to serve as mirrors in which we see ourselves. Different people will reflect different aspects of you, some more reliably than others, so the more widely varied such "mirrors" you consider, the more of yourself you will see and the more accurate the aggregate picture.

- What stories do friends, colleagues, and family tell about you?

206

- Which stories do you enjoy? Why?
- Which stories don't you appreciate? Why?

Exploring Stories You Admire from and about Others

We can learn not only from our own life stories but also from those of others. Furthermore, the practice of considering stories about other people, or the stories they tell, might trigger memories of related experiences in your past.

- Which stories do you admire about other people?
- Which admirable stories have you heard people tell about themselves or others?
- Which stories have inspired you? Why?
- Which stories resonate with you or seem to reveal something about you? Why?
- Do these bring to mind similar stories from your life experience?

Exploring Stories You Want to Live Into

You have a past, which can't be changed. You also have a future, which you can influence by your vision, values, priorities, and choices today.

- In ten years, what life stories do you want to be able to tell?
- What stories do you want friends and family to tell at your funeral?
- Tell a not-yet-true story that you want to make true and that will impact your children and grandchildren.

207

Or that will impact the next generation of leaders who know you.

- Write the epitaph you want on your gravestone. What future stories will ensure this will be true of your life?
- How will these target stories shape your future life and leadership?

Thank You

Thank you for joining me on this journey of finding your unique leadership style. Writing a book is exhilarating, scary, and creates a profound sense of responsibility. I couldn't do it alone. Thanks to those who were integral to this journey.

I am especially grateful to my coach and friend Brad Lomenick; my literary agent, Chris Ferebee; my writing mentors Jonathan Merritt and Margaret Feinberg; my editing and research team at Southwest Michigan First: Heather Baker, Faye Davis, and Jake Fredericks; and the board of directors and the teams at Southwest Michigan First and C2 Consulting (Joe Agostinelli, Damon Allison, Jill Bland, Heather Burnett, Trisha Dunham, Andy Eaton, Jason Evans, Miranda Garside, Justine Griffin, Amanda Harrison, Michael Henry, Cynthia Hernandez, Cathy Knapp, Sarah Mansberger, Kelsey McKague, Paige Niven, Derek Nofz, Brianna Pate, Nick Riashi, Gretchen Slenk, Carla Sones, Petey Stephanak, Kim Weishaar, and Sarah Weishaar), who encouraged me and kept our businesses moving forward while I hid away to write.

To the team at Baker Publishing Group (especially Brian Vos, Chad Allen, Eileen Hanson, and Jennifer Leep) and my editor, Brian Smith: thank you for your belief and support.

Thank you to Andy Stanley and Glen Jackson for giving me the vocabulary for our preeminent journey.

Thanks to the members of my personal board of directors, especially Bill Parfet, Bill Johnston, Marc Schupan, Raghu Elluru, Joe Adame, Gene Guernsey, and Mark Scott.

To my brother, John Kitchens, and mother, Judy Williams: thank you for allowing me to share our stories.

And to my wife, Lyn, and daughter, Kelsey: you are my alpha and omega.

I am so grateful that you would allow me to join you on your journey. If I can assist you or you want to talk about anything in this book, reach out at ron@ronkitchens.com or call me on my direct line at (269) 217-9831.

Always forward.

Ron

Our 4:40 Review

Southwest Michigan First uses the following two-page form for team member reviews every forty days. You can read more about our process in chapter 10.

4:40

name:	mentor partner:	date:

Individual annual goals/updates		

How are you doing against your goals?	

What are your top 5 Gallup strengths and are you using them?	1.	
	2.	
	3.	
	4.	
	5.	

What should I know?	

Four areas of focus/ updates	1.	3.
	2.	4.

How are you doing against your leadership-level responsibilities?		GOOD				BAD
	Profit and loss responsibilities	◯	◯	◯	◯	◯
	Direct report to senior partner	◯	◯	◯	◯	◯
	Lead staff/team members (including development team members)	◯	◯	◯	◯	◯
	Public leadership/organizational spokesperson	◯	◯	◯	◯	◯
	State and/or national profile as thought leader	◯	◯	◯	◯	◯
	Innovating strategic organizational growth	◯	◯	◯	◯	◯
	Assigned Board of Director relationships	◯	◯	◯	◯	◯

What do you need to succeed?

How are you doing against your leadership-level responsibilities?

Meetings with assigned board members	
Key issues	
Percent attending meetings	
Other comments	

Personal commitment

Name	Mentor Partner

213

Lyn and Ron's Original Goals

Read chapter 19 for more about my and Lyn's goals (see also appendix C).

- ☑ Be able to buy more than one week's worth of toilet paper at a time.
- ☑ Be able to buy a tire without it being a crisis.
- ☑ Own a home nice enough to host the governor.
- ☑ Own a brand-new car.
- ☑ Have a career, not just a job.
- ☐ Have dinner at the White House.
- ☑ Own a boat.
- ☑ Have our kids never know scarcity.
- ☑ Own a ranch to hold big charity events. (It ended up being a lake house.)
- ☑ Shop at the grocery stores without needing coupons.
- ☑ Never divorce. (Twenty-nine years and counting.)

Ron's Current Goals

☐ Have retirement fully funded by 12/31/2030.

☐ Serve on a board of a midsized company that does business nationally.

☐ Quail hunt three times per year.

☐ Have two fully committed vacations per year with Lyn.

☐ Have dinner at the White House.

☐ Own a second home in the South.

☐ Mentor fifty people who go on to lead their own organizations.

☐ Donate one hundred thousand cans of mandarin oranges to food banks.

Notes

Chapter 2 "You Can't Read"

1. Andrew Perrin, "Who Doesn't Read Books in America?" *Pew Research Center*, March 23, 2018, http://www.pewresearch.org/fact-tank /2018/03/23/who-doesnt-read-books-in-america.
2. Original source unknown; commonly misattributed to Mark Twain. See https://quoteinvestigator.com/2012/12/11/cannot-read.
3. Perrin, "Who Doesn't Read Books in America?"
4. Charlie Munger, as quoted in David Clark, *The Tao of Charlie Munger: A Compilation of Quotes from Berkshire Hathaway's Vice Chairman on Life, Business, and the Pursuit of Wealth* (New York: Scribner, 2017), 193.

Chapter 3 Lunch Shaming

1. Bettina Elias Siegel, "Shaming Children So Parents Will Pay the School Lunch Bill," *New York Times*, April 30, 2017, https://www.ny times.com/2017/04/30/well/family/lunch-shaming-children-parents -school-bills.html.

Chapter 4 Pork Chops

1. Mark Twain, *Innocents Abroad* (London: Collins, 1869), 243.

Chapter 6 "I Know You Can"

1. Ralph Waldo Emerson, as quoted in Maria Popova, "Incomparable Things Said Incomparably Well: Emerson's Extraordinary Letter of

Appreciation to Young Walt Whitman," *Brain Pickings*, September 8, 2014, https://www.brainpickings.org/2014/09/08/emerson-whitman-letter.

Chapter 12 Surround Yourself

1. Jim Rohn (@OfficialJimRohn), Facebook post, September 6, 2014, https://www.facebook.com/OfficialJimRohn/posts/you-are-the-average-of-the-five-people-you-spend-the-most-time-with-jim-rohn/10154545230540635.

2. David McClelland, as paraphrased in Sam Hazledine, "Five Steps to Creating a Peer Group That Lifts You Up," *MedWorld*, accessed August 28, 2018, http://www.medworld.org/surround_yourself_by_people_who_fill_you_up_not_empty_you.

3. Henry Ford, as quoted in Mike Henry, *What They Didn't Teach You in American History Class: The Second Encounter* (London: Rowman & Littlefield, 2016), 124.

4. Isaac Newton, *Principia, A Revision of Motte's Translation by F. Cajori* (Berkeley: University of California Press, 1934), 13.

Chapter 14 CEO of Your Own Responsibilities

1. David Ogilvy, as quoted in Rich Karlgaard, "Hire Bigger Than You Are," *Forbes*, July 2, 2009, https://www.forbes.com/2009/07/02/karlgaard-leadership-hiring-intelligent-technology-ogilvy.html.

2. Steve Jobs, as quoted in Rama Dev Jager and Rafael Ortiz, *In the Company of Giants: Candid Conversations with the Visionaries of the Digital World* (New York: McGraw-Hill, 1998), 12.

3. Ritz-Carlton, "Gold Standards," Ritz-Carlton, accessed October 17, 2017, http://www.ritzcarlton.com/en/about/gold-standards.

4. Ibid.

5. Blake Mycoskie, *Start Something That Matters* (New York: Spiegel & Grau, 2012), 136.

Chapter 15 Family First

1. Robert Rietbroek, as quoted in Frank Chung, "Why PepsiCo CEO Asks His Team to 'Leave Loudly,'" *Daily Telegraph*, September 12, 2017, https://www.dailytelegraph.com.au/business/work/why-pepsico-ceo-asks-his-team-to-leave-loudly/news-story/5467b3ffff387c3a5dd79ac3a245c868.

2. Casey Stengel, as quoted in Daniel Wyatt, "Wyatt: Casey Stengel Was No Clown," Society for American Baseball Research, July 14, 2014, https://sabr.org/latest/wyatt-casey-stengel-was-no-clown.

3. Jeff Bennett, "Class Act," *Wall Street Journal*, July 28, 2008, https://www.wsj.com/articles/SB121676435398175079.

4. "The Best Places to Work: 2016," *Outside*, November 15, 2016, https://www.outsideonline.com/2134736/best-places-work-2016.

5. "Elite Winners," Best and Brightest, accessed June 9, 2018, https://thebestandbrightest.com/events/2017-best-brightest-companies-work-nation/winners/?winyear=352.

Chapter 16 Be Original

1. Tom Peters, "The Brand Called You," *Fast Company*, August 31, 1997, https://www.fastcompany.com/28905/brand-called-you.

2. Zig Ziglar, *Secrets of Closing the Sale* (Grand Rapids: Revell, 1984), 26.

Chapter 17 Action over Emotion

1. Dale Carnegie, as quoted in "High Impact Presentations: Course Overview," Dale Carnegie, accessed September 10, 2018, https://www.dalecarnegie.com/en/courses/high-impact-presentation.

2. Paulo Coelho, *The Alchemist* (New York: HarperCollins, 1993), 141.

3. Louisa May Alcott, *Little Women* (repr. Seattle: Amazon Classics, 2017), 541.

4. George Patton, as quoted in Porter B. Williamson, *General Patton's Principles for Life and Leadership* (Tucson: Management & Systems Consultants, 1979), 81.

5. W. Clement Stone, as quoted in John Maxwell, "What Are Your Fears Keeping You From Doing?" John Maxwell Co., January 10, 2011, http://www.johnmaxwell.com/blog/what-are-your-fears-keeping-you-from-doing.

Chapter 18 Protecting Joy

1. Sherrie Bourg Carter, "The Tell Tale Signs of Burnout . . . Do You Have Them?" *Psychology Today*, November 26, 2013, https://www.psychologytoday.com/us/blog/high-octane-women/201311/the-tell-tale-signs-burnout-do-you-have-them.

2. Llamo Dhondup (fourteenth Dalai Lama), as quoted in Pearl Marshall and Margaret Studer, "Enthroned at 4, Exiled at 23, Tibet's Dalai Lama Visits the U.S., but Can He Go Home Again?" *People*, September 10, 1979, https://people.com/archive/enthroned-at-4-exiled-at-23-tibets-dalai-lama-visits-the-u-s-but-can-he-go-home-again-vol-12-no-11.

3. Peter Drucker, as quoted in Jennifer Porter, "Why You Should Make Time for Self-Reflection (Even If You Hate Doing It)," *Harvard Business Review*, March 21, 2017, https://hbr.org/2017/03/why-you-should-make -time-for-self-reflection-even-if-you-hate-doing-it.

4. Jim Collins, *Good to Great: Why Some Companies Make the Leap and Others Don't* (New York: HarperCollins, 2001), 1.

5. Jon Acuff (@JonAcuff), Twitter post, May 19, 2018, https://twitter .com/JonAcuff/status/997897327401750529.

6. Paul Rasmussen, "Transcript of Video Sermon Podcast," Highland Park United Methodist Church, October 18, 2015, http://www.hpumc .org/mediafiles/cornerstone-video-podcast.xml.

Chapter 19 What Do You Want?

1. *City Slickers*, written by Lowell Ganz and Babaloo Mandel, di- rected by Ron Underwood (1991; Los Angeles: Castle Rock Entertain- ment, 2015), DVD.

Chapter 20 The Kindness of Candor

1. *Cool Hand Luke*, written by Donn Pearce and Frank R. Pierson, directed by Stuart Rosenberg (1967; Beverly Hills: Jalem Productions, 2008), DVD.

2. Ed Catmull, *Creativity, Inc.: Overcoming the Unseen Forces That Stand in the Way of True Inspiration* (New York: Random House, 2014), Kindle loc. 4747–56.

3. Catmull, *Creativity, Inc.*, Kindle loc. 1473–87.

Chapter 21 Love Notes

1. Oprah Winfrey, as quoted in Kevin Daum, "Twenty-Three Oprah Quotes That Inspire a Better Life," *Inc.*, March 9, 2017, https://www .inc.com/kevin-daum/23-oprah-quotes-that-inspire-a-better-life.html.

2. Douglas R. Conant, "Secrets of Positive Feedback," *Harvard Business Review*, February 16, 2011, https://hbr.org/2011/02/secrets-of -positive-feedback.

3. Gary Trust, "Taylor Swift Sends Cardi B Flowers After 'Bodak Yellow' Hits No. 1 on Hot 100," *Billboard*, September 25, 2017, https:// www.billboard.com/articles/news/7980814/taylor-swift-cardi-b-flowers -instagram-bodak-yellow.

4. Tom Peters (@tom_peters), Twitter post, December 27, 2017, https:// twitter.com/tom_peters/status/946008821314539521.

5. Y. Joel Wong et al., "Does Gratitude Writing Improve the Mental Health of Psychotherapy Clients? Evidence from a Randomized Controlled

Trial," *Psychotherapy Research*, vol. 28, no. 2 (May 3, 2016): 192–202, https://www.tandfonline.com/doi/abs/10.1080/10503307.2016.1169332?journalCode=tpsr20.

6. Gary Chapman, *The Five Languages of Appreciation in the Workplace* (Chicago: Northfield Publishing, 2011), 5.

7. Stillman St. Clair and Melissa Van Dyke, "Recognition Remains Important in a Diverse and Evolving Workforce," *Insight*, vol. 7 (2007): 1, https://www.maritz.com/~/media/Files/MaritzDotCom/White%20Papers/Motivation/Recognition-Remains-Important-in-a-Diverse-and-Evolving-Workforce.pdf.

8. William James, *The Principles of Psychology*, vol. 1 (repr. New York: Cosimo, 2007), 293.

Chapter 23 Scrum

1. Robert Orben, "Quips & Quotes," *Rome News-Tribune*, July 28, 1974, 19.

Chapter 24 The Four Most Powerful Words

1. Mark Batterson, *Chase the Lion* (New York: Random House, 2016), 156.

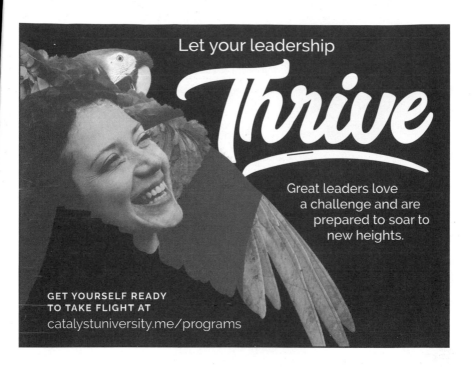

Ron Kitchens is the senior partner and chief executive officer of Southwest Michigan First, which has been named by *Outside Magazine* and the *Wall Street Journal* as one of the best places to work. One of America's leading thinkers on business, leadership, and entrepreneurialism, Ron is the founder of the leadership conference Catalyst University and the cofounder of NEXT, an invitation-only leadership symposium for global economic development leaders. Ron and his teams have been extensively featured in more than one hundred national and international media outlets, including the *Wall Street Journal*, *Fast Company*, CBS, NBC, Fox, *USA Today*, *Forbes*, *Fortune*, *The Economist*, and NPR. Ron is author or coauthor of three books, including *Community Capitalism*. He blogs and podcasts at www.ronkitchens.com and can be found on Twitter @ronkitchens.